Options Trading for Beginners, Dummies & Idiots

By Giovanni Rigters

© Copyright 2021 - All rights reserved.

The contents of this book may not be reproduced, duplicated or transmitted without direct written permission from the author.

Under no circumstances will any legal responsibility or blame be held against the publisher for any reparation, damages, or monetary loss due to the information herein, either directly or indirectly.

Legal Notice:

This book is copyright protected. This is only for personal use. You cannot amend, distribute, sell, use, quote or paraphrase any part or the content within this book without the consent of the author.

Disclaimer Notice:

Please note the information contained within this document is for educational and entertainment purposes only. Every attempt has been made to provide accurate, up to date and reliable complete information. No warranties of any kind are expressed or implied. Readers acknowledge that the author is not engaging in the rendering of legal, financial, medical or professional advice. The content of this book has been derived from various sources. Please consult a licensed professional before attempting any techniques outlined in this book.

By reading this document, the reader agrees that under no circumstances is the author responsible for any losses, direct or indirect, which are incurred as a result of the use of information contained within this document, including, but not limited to, — errors, omissions, or inaccuracies.

Table of Contents

Introduction

Chapter 1: Stepping into the World of Options
Brief History of Options Trading
What Is Options Trading?
Basic Terminology
Types of Options

Chapter 2: Why Trade Options?
Benefits of Options Trading
Beware of Options Trading Myths

Chapter 3: How Are Options Priced?

Chapter 4: Strategic Planning
The Advantages of Having a Trading Strategy
Steps to Follow

Chapter 5: How to Select a Trading Strategy
Start With Your Outlook
Consider the Risk
Using Spreads
Number of Trades
The Complexity of the Strategy

Chapter 6: Trading Strategies for Beginners
Bearish Outlook
Bullish Outlook

Neutral Outlook

Volatile Outlook

Chapter 7: Strategies for Bears

Long Put

Short Call

Bear Put Spread

Bear Call Spread

Bear Ratio Spread

Short Bear Ratio Spread

Bear Butterfly Spread

Bear Put Ladder Spread

Chapter 8: Strategies for Bulls

Long Call

Short Put

Bull Call Spread

Bull Put Spread

Bull Ratio Spread

Short Bull Spread

Bull Butterfly Spread

Bull Condor Spread

Bull Call Ladder Spread

Chapter 9: Trading in a Neutral Market

Covered Call

Covered Put

Covered Call Collar

Short Straddle
Short Gut
Short Strangle
Calendar Call Spread
Call Ratio Spread
Calendar Put Spread
Put Ratio Spread
Calendar Straddle
Calendar Strangle
Butterfly Spread
Short Iron Butterfly Spread
Iron Albatross Spread
Condor Spread

Chapter 10: Trading in a Volatile Market

Long Straddle
Long Strangle
Strip Straddle
Strip Strangle
Strap Strangle
Strap Straddle
Call Ratio Backspread
Put Ratio Backspread
Short Calendar Call Spread
Short Calendar Put Spread
Short Butterfly Spread

Short Condor Spread
Reverse Iron Butterfly Spread
Reverse Iron Condor Spread

Chapter 11: Selecting Options to Trade
Investment Goals
Risk Tolerance
Implied Volatility
Different Events
Create a Strategy

Chapter 12: How to Select a Broker
Learning Opportunities
Customer Service
Tools and Resources
Trading Platform
Commission Payable

Chapter 13: Before Entering a Trade
Start With a Balanced Portfolio
Liquidity
Implied Volatility
Select a Strategy
Personal Trading Style
Position Size
The Future

Chapter 14: Mistakes to Avoid

Acquiring Out of the Money Calls
Always Have an Exit Plan
Liquidity
Don't Double Down
Multiple Trades
Misunderstanding Leverage
Not Trying New Strategies
Waiting Too Long
Not Considering Upcoming Events

Chapter 15: Managing Emotions
Fear of Missing Out
Learn to Be Patient
Be Willing to Learn
A Sense of Direction
Don't Rush

Chapter 16: Risk Management
A Trading Plan
Different Orders
Diversify the Portfolio
Automate Orders

Conclusion

References

Introduction

There are many options available in investing, including stocks, bonds, and even real estate. These are all conventional, but there is another extremely profitable instrument that is commonly overlooked: options. Options belong to a class of instruments known as derivatives, and they have an entire ecosystem of their own.

There are popular misconceptions out there, like trading in options is risky. The truth is, options offer incredible levels of profitability, unlike any other trading instruments. All you need to do is understand what they are, how they operate, and the different strategies you can use to leverage the prevalent conditions in the market.

Change and development have become constant in the global world, and the investment market is no different. These days, an average investor has greater access to different financial instruments than ever before. Enter options trading.

Many commodity traders prefer to trade in options because of all the advantages it offers. Of the major ones is you cannot lose more capital than you have invested. These instruments are flexible and versatile, their risk and reward ratio are higher than other instruments, and learning to trade in options is incredibly interesting and exciting.

In this book, you will learn about the brief history of options, what options trading means, different options, and the basic terminology associated with this instrument.

You will learn about the different benefits of options trading, the risks involved, and the popular myths you must ignore while trading. Once you get the hang of the basics, we will delve into the different market outlooks, factors to consider while selecting a trading strategy, and different trading strategies.

This book will also introduce you to other essential topics associated with trading options. These include risk management, selecting the right broker, making smart investments, some common mistakes to avoid, and tips to increase your overall profitability.

Once you are armed with all the information in this book, you can start trading in options easily. So, step into the world of options trading and become a successful trader! Whether you want to improve your finances or are curious about learning how this instrument works, this book has everything you need! Let's get started immediately!

Chapter 1: Stepping into the World of Options

Calls, puts, strike price, American options...

What do all these terms mean? If you are new to the world of options, it can be slightly intimidating and overwhelming, but you will get the hang of it soon enough. In this chapter, you will learn about options and their history, how options trading works, and the basic terminology associated with it.

Brief History of Options Trading

Understanding the history of options will make it easier for you to perceive how options are traded these days. The first known options trade dates to 350 B.C.E. Thales of Miletus, a Greek mathematician, is believed to be the first option buyer. One season, he predicted the olive harvest would be greater than usual. Based on this belief, he approached the press owners and purchased the rights to use their presses during the olive harvest.

He immediately gave the press owners a premium as a lock-in amount to show good faith to reserve his right to use the presses later. The remainder of the predetermined price to use the presses would be paid during the harvest season, as per their agreement. Spring rolled in, and his prediction turned out to be spot on. Since time is of the essence in the olive trade, the farmers were in a rush to reach the presses. However, Thales exercised his right to operate the presses and charged them a higher amount.

This is how an options contract works.

The tulip bubble of the 1630s is an exceptional example of an options trade. The value of tulips started increasing in Holland during the 1630s. The price of Tulip bulbs increased to levels that were neither reasonable nor sustainable. It's quite similar to the .com bubble the world witnessed during the early 2000s.

The perfect market for futures and options was created in the Tulip market because of this simple fact - the bulbs planted by the Tulip dealers wouldn't be ready for sale or delivery immediately and would be deliverable only in the future.

So, this gave buyers a chance to speculate the future price of Tulip bulbs. Because of this, they started agreeing to purchase bulbs at the price when they would be ready for sale in the future. In exchange for this right, the buyers paid the sellers a premium to seal the deal. By paying a small premium, the speculators had the leverage to enter into dozens of contracts to sell Tulip bulbs, so they were acquired at a higher price later. This resulted in the Tulip mania.

Unfortunately, bubbles are not sustainable. The prices came crashing down, and the economy collapsed. Because the futures and options market wasn't regulated, most buyers and sellers shrugged away from their contracts and gave up on their obligations.

Compared to stocks, options became a fully regulated investment only in the 1970s in the United States. Before 1973, the options market was incredibly chaotic because option buyers entered into individual contracts with the sellers. Since the terms of every contract were different, there were several standardizations.

Once standardization of stock options took place, one contract was believed to be equivalent to one hundred shares of stock. Apart from this, the contract's expiration date, strike price, and size were also standardized. The Chicago Board Options Exchange (CBOE) was the first exchange to trade in listed options within the US.

Call-option trading was offered in over sixteen stocks by CBOE initially. The Securities and Exchange Commission created the Options Clearing Corporation (OCC) to function as the clearinghouse for all options traded on exchanges in 1975. We have certainly come a long way since the first options contract was created and executed. These days, it is a fully regulated market. Once you understand how options and their execution work, trading will become simple.

You will learn more about the basic terminology used in the options market in later sections.

What Is Options Trading?

While talking about investments, the first thing that comes to mind is trading in stocks. The stock market includes different financial instruments investors can actively use for trading. One of these is options.

Options trading is based on the purchase and sale of call and put contracts that are publicly traded on exchanges at a specific price within a specific timeframe. Options are legally binding contracts giving the holder of the option the authority to sell or buy a specific number of underlying securities at a predefined price before the contract expires.

Options are varied and versatile and help mitigate the risk of an investment portfolio. Once you understand how to trade in options, you can also diversify your portfolio while creating an additional income stream.

Options can be used for creating a stream of recurring income or for speculating in the market. Speculation works, especially when you are intuitive when it comes to how stocks will perform. Options are versatile instruments because they involve two parties and are two-sided.

Any basic options contract is the 100 underlying shares of a specific company known as the security. As a buyer, you are obligated to pay a predefined premium or fee upfront for each contract you want to execute.

Before you jump into trading with options, there are plenty of considerations, especially regarding how and where to invest. Options contracts can be used to speculate the price movement for specific stocks, commodities, indices, and foreign commodities as well.

So, the number of opportunities available to invest and trade automatically increases. When this happens, the profitability also increases. The versatility of options and the different types of orders that can be placed cannot be overlooked.

Whenever you trade in stocks, there are only two ways to earn money. You can either participate in short or long-term trading. When it comes to options, multiple choices are available as to how you want to make the trades. You must spend time carefully studying and learning the various aspects of trading options. The good news is that it is not at all difficult.

Now, this brings us to what an option truly means. Options are derivatives because their value is based on an underlying security. This is what all the option contracts are based on. For instance, ketchup is obtained from tomatoes. So, it is safe to consider ketchup as a derivative of tomatoes.

Using the same logic, a stock option is the derivative of all the underlying shares it is based on. Options are derivatives, and their value depends on the price of another commodity or an asset. The derivative market consists of different types of investments known as futures, forwards, swaps, and options.

Basic Terminology

To become an options trader, learning the basic jargon and terms used in the trade is important. Trading in options and understanding the strategies involved becomes easier once you understand the terms discussed in this section.

Put Option

The buyer of an options contract has the right to sell underlying securities at a fixed price or a strike price with a put option before the contract expires. You have the right to sell stock at a predetermined price within a specific period. The market value of an option is known as the premium.

This is the price paid to acquire the rights provided by a call option. Upon expiration, if the value of the underlying asset is less than their strike price, the premium paid upfront is a loss incurred by the buyer of the call. They are under no obligation to purchase the stock for anything more than the existing market value of the stock.

Upon expiration, if the value is more than the strike price, the buyer can acquire shares at a price less than the market value to earn a profit. You will learn more about the strike price later.

Call Option

Unlike a put option, while executing a call option, you have the right to purchase stock at a predetermined price within a given timeframe. The writer or seller of a call option is obligated to sell the underlying security at a predetermined price if the option is exercised. The writer of the call is obligated to deliver stock or shares while being paid to take on the risk associated with the same.

Exercising the Option

If the holder of an options contract decides to invoke the basic conditions, it is known as exercising the option. Whenever a trader exercises an option, they can purchase the underlying stock if it is a call option.

On the other hand, the put owner has the right to sell the underlying asset based on the terms already determined by the options contract. All options contracts with an intrinsic value of at least one cent are automatically exercised on the date of expiration.

Strike Price

The strike price is one of the most important aspects of options trading. This price refers to the value at which a trader can either buy or sell the underlying asset or stock. The strike price is not only predetermined, but it stays fixed until the contract expires. While exercising options contract, the underlying security, stock, or asset can be purchased or sold only at the strike price.

Hedging

Hedging is associated with reducing the risk of investments. It's a common tactic wherein the investor or trader implements a specific transaction to offset an existing position he holds in the market.

Date of Expiration

A primary feature of the options market is that there is always a date of expiry for each option contract. This is the duration during which an options contract can be exercised by its holder. If a stock option is listed every month, it stops trading up on the third Friday of every month and expires the next day. If it's a weekly option, it expires on Friday of the concerned week.

Intrinsic Value

The intrinsic value refers to the profit you can earn on an options contract if the option is exercised at a certain moment and the underlying asset is either purchased or sold at the existing market price. If the options contract has positive intrinsic value, it means it is in the money. On the other hand, the option is said to be out of the money if it has a negative intrinsic value. You will learn more about both of these terms later.

Time Decay

All options contracts have an expiration date. This is one of the reasons why they are known as wasting assets. Their time value reduces to zero once they expire. This reduction in value is known as time decay. It simply means, as the expiry date of a specific option approaches, its rate of time decay increases.

Time Value

All the options contracts include time value. It is one of the most important factors that regulate the price of an option when it expires. Time value refers to a specific amount where the market price of an option is more than its intrinsic value. To obtain time value, you need to subtract the intrinsic value of an option from its existing market value.

Premium

The costs incurred to obtain an option are known as its premium. The premium includes its intrinsic value and the time value. The primary difference between the strike price and the existing market value of an underlying security or stock is the intrinsic value of an option. Before the option expires, its value is based on the time value for a given period.

Bid Price

The specific amount a buyer is willing to pay to obtain a specific option is known as the bid price. If a trader is selling an options contract, it is the premium he will receive on sale.

Ask Price

The sum a seller is willing to accept in return for an options contract is the asking price. If a trader wants to purchase an option, it is the premium a buyer pays to obtain the contract.

Strike Price

The strike price is the sum a trader either pays or receives when the option is exercised.

Contract Name

All stocks have different symbols, and it is the same for options as well. A contract name includes letters, symbols, and numbers corresponding to all the details present within the contract.

Volatility

Volatility is the maximum change in the value of stocks between high and low prices; a change in the daily prices of a given stock. When all the past pricing data of a specific option is put together, it's known as historical volatility. You can measure it for a specific timeframe or decide to measure it annually too. Implied volatility determines the changes which specific underlying security will experience in the market.

This brings us to another aspect of volatility known as implied volatility. The value of options is determined by their implied volatility. If the implied that when volatility is high, the value of an option will also be high.

Once again, these are all just projections because there is no guarantee when it comes to trading instruments in the market. It is a prediction of how an analyst believes the value of options contracts will be in the market or how its value might change.

Out of the Money

If there is absolutely no financial gain whatsoever left to be obtained when an option contract is exercised, such an option is said to be out of the money. Buying and selling shares at a strike price doesn't seem promising, especially when compared to purchasing or selling in an open market if the option contract expires out of the money.

A call option is out of the money if the current price of the underlying security is lower than its strike price. On the other hand, a put option is out of the money if its strike price is less than the current price in the market at the date of its expiration.

In The Money

A contract is said to be in the money if it has an intrinsic value associated with it. This highlights the relationship between the strike price and the current market value of an underlying security. The owner of a call option will earn a profit if the strike price is less than the existing market value. If the strike price is higher than the current market value of the put option, it is said to be in the money.

At The Money

An options contract is said to be "at-the-money" if its strike price is the same as the current market value for the underlying security or asset.

Holder

The trader or investor who is holding an options contract is the holder. He is the owner of the options contract. The holder of a put contract has the right to sell underlying assets or stock. On the other hand, the holder of a call option has the right to purchase underlying security according to predetermined conditions included in the options contract.

Writer

Options writers are investors selling the option contracts. The options writer receives a premium from the holder in exchange for a promise to either sell or purchase the underlying security at a strike price already decided upon by the holder if they decide to exercise the option. The primary difference between the option holder and writer is their risk exposure.

An option holder is purchasing the right to either buy or sell underlying security or stock. They are under no obligation to do anything. The options contract gives them the required freedom to decide whether they want to exercise the option or sell it before its expiration.

If the holder's option contract expires out of the money, they can walk away from it and let the contract simply expire. It means the loss they incur is just the capital invested and any commission paid to the broker.

On the other hand, an option writer doesn't have such flexibility. For instance, if an option call holder decides to exercise their option before the expiration, the writer should fulfill this order and sell the security at an agreed strike price.

If the options contract is based on a specific stock and the writer doesn't have sufficient stock or shares to sell, they need to purchase the said security or stocks and sell them to the call holder because they have a legally binding obligation to sell.

Spend some time and carefully go through all these terms because they will be used frequently in the subsequent chapters. Unless you thoroughly understand what each of the terms means, you cannot make much sense of the different strategies discussed in this book.

Types of Options

There are different types of options available in the derivatives market. In this section, you will be introduced to the primary types.

Stock Options

These options are exclusive privileges that are sold by one party to another and gives the buyer the right to either purchase or sell a stock at a predetermined price within a given timeframe. A stock option is a legally binding contract between the two parties. It usually represents one hundred underlying shares of a specific stock of a company. Stock options can be either call or put options.

If the buyer agrees to buy a specific stock at a predetermined strike price within a given period, it is known as a call option. On the other hand, if the buyer issues a contract giving the right to sell stock at a specific strike price either before or on the date of expiration, it is known as a put option.

The general idea is that the holder or the buyer of the call option believes that the stock price will increase in the future. However, the seller believes the stock price will reduce. This is how they each earn a profit on the contracts. If the price of the stock doesn't increase and the contract expires, the holder of the option will be profitable.

This happens because he managed to buy the stock when it was trading at a lower price. On the other hand, if the buyer believes the stock price will reduce, he can write a put option contract to sell the stock later. If the stock depreciates before expiration, the option holder can sell the stock in exchange for a premium.

The primary factor that determines the value of an option in all these situations is its strike price. While executing options contracts, remember the strike price is always predetermined.

The call option holder will profit only if the strike price is lower in comparison to the existing value of the underlying security in the market. On the other hand, the holder of put options profits only when the strike price is more than the existing value of the underlying security.

It's a common misconception that stock options are the same as employee stock options. Employee stock options don't have a specific maturity date, unlike regular stock options. Whenever an employee works at the same company for a specific period, he's eligible to purchase stock options in said company.

Instead of the strike price, which is associated with stock options, employee stock options offer a grant price. The grant price represents the value of the stock at the time the employee received them.

Binary Options

The simplest form of options you can trade these days are binary options. They are based on a binary proposal of either yes or no. It's one simple question the investor needs to answer while selecting the options. The question is about determining whether the value of the underlying security or asset will be greater than a specific amount at a given time or not.

The trader must answer this question with either a yes or no. Depending on this answer, he can start trading. There are no complicated calculations involved here. This is one of the reasons why binary options are considered to be incredibly easy to understand and simple to trade.

Even though it sounds extremely simple and appealing to new traders, it's important to understand all the benefits and risks associated with them. Before you start trading, it is important to understand that the price of binary options does not exceed $100. While trading, you must be aware of the bid price and offer price.

The bid price is the amount the buyer is willing to pay for a specific option, and the asking price or offer price is the sum a seller is willing to accept instead of an option.

Here is a simple example of how binary trading works. Will the price of silver increase over $1000 at 1:30 PM on a specific day or not? If, as a trader, you believe it will, you need to purchase binary options at that offer price. If you think the price will not increase, you will need to sell your binary options at a sum lower than the offer price. If the value of silver exceeds $1000 at 1:30 PM, the option will expire, and you stand to profit from it. On the other hand, if the price reduces, all the money invested in the option will be lost.

Index Options

Financial derivatives are usually based on stock indexes such as Dow Jones Industrial Average or the S&P 500. Index options share similarities with stock options as they also provide the investor with the privilege of either purchasing or selling a stock index within a fixed timeframe.

Index options can be in the form of either American or European options. As an investor, you have the opportunity to exercise your right to either sell or purchase the stock before expiration while using American options. On the other hand, if you are using European options, this right to either purchase or sell the underlying stock cannot be exercised until the option expires.

The benefits offered by index options are the same as stock options. They also have the added advantage of offering exposure to a variety of securities. Instead of focusing solely on the stocks of a single company, an index option lets you invest in stocks of different companies.

Unlike stock options that are settled through deliverables, index options are settled only by cash.

The strike price and the premium of index options are expressed in terms of points.

Short Term Options

As the name suggests, any option with a brief expiry period is known as a short-term option. The duration of these options can range from one week to a couple of months and is influenced by the country of issuance. Short-term options are also used in intraday trading wherein the period is either a single day or a week.

If you are just getting started with trading, opt for these options. They are a quick study because, as a trader, you can apply all your theoretical knowledge and gain expertise. It also means you don't have to wait for weeks together to see the results of the trade decisions you make. A disadvantage is that the value of the underlying securities might not drastically change due to the restricted time frame.

In case of a loss, the trader hardly has an opportunity to recover from the position and will, therefore, need to accept the loss. This is not the case with long-term investments, where a prolonged time frame allows investors to see whether or not the market conditions will change.

By investing in short-term options, you can sell them at any point before their expiry date and earn a profit. To make the most of short-term options, you must understand the basic concepts involved in options trading. To become a successful trader, look for different stock options in which you can invest. Start by observing the trading patterns, general trends in the market, trader sentiments toward a specific stock, and the moving averages. Apart from this, you should also perform a technical analysis to understand whether the underlying stocks or securities will perform well or not.

Long-Term Options

As the name suggests, any option held for prolonged periods of time is known as a long-term option. They are usually held for one year or more. If you purchase a call option on Feb 1st, 2020, that expires on Feb 1st, 2021, it is a long-term option. An obvious benefit of trading in long-term options is it lets you capitalize on price movements that will take place over a prolonged time frame.

Even if the value of the underlying asset reduces initially, you have a chance of recovering from any setback. Long-term options are an incredible opportunity for first-time investors, especially those who are interested in studying the market while reducing their risk exposure.

Long-term options are also known as LEAPS (long-term equity anticipation securities). These options are not just available for regular stocks on the market, but for future securities too. Most investors believe that an extra time frame gives them the chance to make calculated decisions about whether they should hold onto the underlying asset or sell their position. For instance, if you are interested in purchasing and holding security, then a long-term investment will be better than a short-term one. On the other hand, a day trader will prefer the short-term due to the brief trading period.

American Options

The American options are incredibly popular and the most commonly used form of options contracts these days. It allows traders to exercise their right of sale at any time from acquiring the option until its expiration. For instance, let's assume you purchased a call option based on the stock of a specific company in December 2020, and this option expires within a month.

Now, as a trader, you have the choice to sell this option contract any time before the one-month period ends. You don't necessarily have to wait until the option has expired in order to exercise your right. If you believe you have a better chance of earning a profit right away, you can sell it immediately instead of waiting for it to expire.

American options are good investment vehicles for those dealing with significant investments in the form of capital in the options market.

It offers investors the right to purchase or sell options according to their preferences. If you sell short, you have the option of purchasing the same option again and selling it once it expires. American options allow you to stay invested in the game for as long as you desire while earning profits.

Another interesting feature of American options is the date of exercising the option. If the American options are exercised every week, the last chance to exercise the option before it expires is Friday of that week.

Similarly, if the American options are traded every month, the last Friday in the last week of the month will be the date when the option expires. Don't be under the misconception that these options are restricted only to the United States because of their name.

American options don't have any geographical constraints or restrictions. They are simply known as such because most of the companies exercising this specific type of option are located in the United States.

European Options

This brings us to the next type of option known as European options. Unlike American options, the level of flexibility offered isn't high. Whenever you are using one, you have the right to sell the option only after it expires.

For instance, say you purchased a call option for underlying security or stocks of a specific company in December 2020, and it expires in December 2021. You have the right to sell only when it expires in

December 2021. The right to exercise the option is available only on the date of expiration. Even if the value of the underlying security skyrockets sometime in the middle of this timeframe, you cannot do anything about it.

You will have to wait until the expiration date to exercise your right. Like American options, European options are also not restricted to regions in Europe. So, don't get confused by their name.

Exotic Options

This category of options includes all options that weren't covered in the previous categories. Exotic options usually come with different privileges and are special. They are commonly favored by high-end investors. These options are quite different from conventional ones in terms of their payment structures, strike prices, and expiry date.

They are hybrid securities of American and European options that are customizable according to the needs of investors or traders, and they fall somewhere between these two types of options. A usual options contract gives the holder the choice to buy or sell the underlying security at a fixed price before or on the expiry date.

Exotic options contracts have no such obligations. The investor has the right to purchase the underlying security using a call option.

Exotic options are usually traded in over-the-counter markets instead of large exchanges such as the New York Stock exchange and are commonly used for trading commodities such as natural gas, lumber and corn. They can also be used for bonds, foreign exchange, and equities.

Chapter 2: Why Trade Options?

Unless you are aware of why you are doing something, the chance of getting things done reduces. This is applicable in all aspects of life. It is especially true when you are trying to learn something new.

Since you are just getting started with trading options, it's important to understand why you want to do this. If you have never given it much thought, now is the time. Learning anything becomes easier when you are aware of the benefits it offers and everything you stand to gain.

If you are still trying to understand why you want to trade options, here are all the different benefits associated with it.

Benefits of Options Trading

Buying and trading stocks is easy to understand and perform. The primary benefit of trading stocks is the profitability it offers. Apart from that, they are also quite common and popular trading instruments. All this changes when it comes to options. Even though they have been around for a while, options have only started gaining popularity recently. However, the benefits they offer cannot be overlooked.

Capital

A primary advantage of trading options is you can focus on attaining significant profits without a massive capital investment. They are an ideal choice for anyone who has a limited budget for investment.

Don't make the mistake of assuming that trading options is a safe and risk-free way to make a quick buck. You can make significant profits with low capital, but it is not risk-free, and it has a learning curve. That said, the profitability offered by options is unlike any other financial tool.

For instance, let's assume that you have $1500. You invested this in a company's stocks that are presently trading at $20 each. You use all your capital to purchase stocks. When you do this, you'll own seventy-five shares of the company.

If the price increases to $25, you earn $5 per share of profit. It means your total profit in this situation is only $375. It's a 25% increase on the original investment you made.

Now, let's consider trading options. If you are purchasing call options for the same stock, let's see how it works. If the call option is available at a strike price of $20 and is trading at $2 per share, you can purchase 75 options. This gives you the right to purchase 750 stocks at the given strike price.

If the strike price increases to $25, you have the option to exercise your right to purchase and acquire all shares. Once you acquire them, you can sell them for their existing value, which is $25 per share. It means you can sell them all for $18750. Even though you started with $1500 in both examples, by trading options, you are left with a profit of $17250. This is a 150% increase on your capital.

This is a basic example of how options trading works. You won't always get such massive returns. That said, the general returns offered by options are quite good. You can make incredibly profitable trades, provided you understand how options work and the different strategies involved.

Flexibility

The flexibility offered by options is unlike any other financial instrument. For starters, it is entirely up to you to invest in options as a form of passive investment or active trading. When it comes to investing in stocks, there are only limited strategies to make the most of.

For instance, if you purchase stocks to create a portfolio and are using a buyer and hold approach, it means there are only two ways the entire investment will play out. You can either purchase stocks, such as data value, which increases with time, or you can concentrate on purchasing stocks that provide regular returns. There isn't much to choose from here. You can even earn from short or long-term investments.

You can combine both strategies, but there are only a few variations associated with them. Based on your risk tolerance, capital, and duration, the strategies will differ. For instance, you can opt for a conventional strategy by only making investments where the risks are limited. On the other hand, you must be willing to take massive risks to earn significant returns.

Even if you want to trade stocks actively, there are restrictions and limitations that cannot be overlooked. You can purchase stocks you believe will appreciate or short sell those that depreciate. Even if you put all these factors together, the flexibility offered by conventional financial instruments isn't as good as the ones offered by options.

Options can be purchased and sold depending on the underlying security. You can also use options to speculate the movement of stock prices or the price movement of any other commodity, including foreign currencies. Even if you only consider these points, it becomes quite obvious that there are several ways to make profitable trades by using options.

For instance, if you have gained knowledge about a specific industry, you can invest in different options for securities belonging to said industry. You are not only investing in stocks but another financial instrument to diversify your overall portfolio. It doesn't get better than this.

As you go through all the different chapters in this book, you will realize there are many strategies applicable to options trading, depending on your outlook of the market. Regardless of whether you want to mitigate your risks, reduce the upfront cost, or earn a profit from price movement in either direction, the options offered were settled. They can be used to hedge any of your existing positions, especially during uncertain market conditions.

Options can also be used to make profits even if the market is stagnant, which is incredibly difficult when trading stocks. Yes, you can earn money in a neutral market as well. This is what sets options apart from other financial instruments.

Rewards Involved

After going through the above-mentioned benefits, you have probably realized that the reward to risk ratio is quite favorable when it comes to options trading for structures due to the cost and capital efficiency it offers. Even with minimal investment, you can obtain significant results. The risk and reward ratio offered is better than any other financial tool.

That said, unless you are using the right strategy, you cannot reap the rewards you desire. It's also equally important to understand that options trading is not risk-free. Just because it offers good returns doesn't mean there is no risk involved with it.

If you want to earn high returns, be prepared to increase your risk tolerance. A wonderful thing about options is you have complete control over your risk exposure while investing or trading. If you take all the different types of options contracts that can be traded and various orders that can be executed into consideration, you can effectively limit the risk exposure of your portfolio. This is one of the benefits options trading offers when compared to stock investments and trades. You will learn more about risk management in later chapters.

Risks Involved

As mentioned, certain risks are involved in the world even when you are trading options. Despite all the advantages they offer, you cannot overlook these. If you want to be a successful investor, it's important to understand the risks in options trading and take corrective action to rectify them. Let's look at all the risks associated with options trading for stock.

Liquidity

Although options trading is steadily gaining popularity, certain issues are still associated with the options market, such as liquidity filter top. There is a variety of options to choose from, and therefore, it's quite likely a certain type of option is only created in small volumes.

In a situation like this, it can become slightly tricky to execute the required trades at the right prices. It is not a significant issue if you are trading with popular options or low volumes. For anyone who wants to trade in high volumes or doesn't want to use mainstream options, the risk of liquidity increases. Liquidity in a market is measured by the number of traders who are interested in transacting in a specific security or asset. If there aren't many people in the market and the ones who are in it are not interested in trading in the option that you want, liquidity will become a problem.

Potential for Losses

Even though trading options offers better profitability and flexibility than other instruments, it also has potential for losses. You can use different strategies to limit your risk exposure or reduce the upfront cost of acquiring and executing options, and you can also determine the maximum of potential loss you might incur. All this information comes in handy while planning trades.

After all that is said and done, the risk associated with investment cannot be overlooked. Regardless of all the experience and knowledge you have, certain factors will always be beyond your control. Even seasoned investors make mistakes, and therefore, it's important to understand the different types of risks you are exposed to while trading.

Whenever you use the leverage offered by options, you have a chance to increase the buying power of your capital. For instance, if you purchase call options, reward $500 based on the underlying security of stock of a specific company. After this, you earn a profit that is more than the amount invested.

If the value of the stock reduces or crashes, the call options will expire worthlessly, and the entire capital you invested will be lost. Here, had you just invested the $500 in the stock of the said company, you wouldn't have lost your entire capital unless the company had gone bankrupt.

This is a rather simple point that most investors fail to consider when trading in options. If you want to become a good investor, you must be aware of the strengths and weaknesses associated with the instruments you opt to trade in. That said, certain steps can be taken to reduce this risk. For instance, you can establish stop-loss orders or create a spread. You will learn more about all of these later.

Time Decay

And the unavoidable risk of trading and options is the time decay associated with different types of options. The longer you wait, or the closer the option is to its expiration, the higher its time decay will be. Any option you hold tends to lose a little of its value. It doesn't necessarily mean the entire value will depreciate over time. That said, the negative effect of time decay cannot be overlooked.

Complexities

Whenever you are trading in options, you cannot forget the complexities that are involved. This is also a risk you must consider. Understanding the basics of options trading is easy. That said, certain trading aspects, especially advanced strategies, are not that easy to understand. It becomes even more complicated when simultaneous transactions need to be executed for different positions you want to hold in the market. Do not make the mistake of making trades or assuming positions you don't understand. Unless you have a thorough understanding of the market and the instrument you are investing in, don't go ahead with the option.

If you are not careful here, you might end up hurting your financial health. It's quite easy to start second-guessing yourself, especially if it's a new concept or topic. The good news is that a little practice and willingness to learn will help overcome this limitation as well.

Costs

The liquidity of the option determines the costs involved in trading them. The price of any options contract includes bid and ask price. The sum received for writing an option is the bid price. The price paid to purchase an option is the asking price. The asking price is usually higher than the bid price.

The difference between these two helps spread and is known as the bid-ask spread. The spread is also an indirect cost that you must consider while trading options. The wider the spread, the higher the cost. At times, the lack of liquidity in the market can result in bigger spreads than you planned.

When you compare this with other forms of investment, the commission charged by a broker and the direct cost of trading is a little high with options. When it comes to trading instruments, certain calls are unavoidable. So, don't forget to factor in all these different costs before you make a trade.

Creating an option spread has several advantages. One of the most obvious ones is when you are simultaneously executing multiple contracts, you save the upfront costs order fees payable. Once again, the commission payable will depend on the broker or brokerage service you are using.

Beware of Options Trading Myths

Perhaps the most common misconception about options trading is that it is extremely risky. Well, to be fair, the risk exists in everything you do, and investments are no different. There is a certain degree of risk associated with every investment you make.

The same applies to options trading as well. After all, unless you are willing to take some risks, you cannot earn rewards. However, you have complete control over your level of risk exposure. In this section, let's look at some popular misconceptions about options trading.

Trading in Options is a Zero-sum Game

Trading is not a zero-sum game. If you believe otherwise, it's nothing more than a misconception.

Traders usually use youth options as insurance policies or for reducing their risk exposure. Options are also financial tools, and they can be traded like any other instrument in an investment portfolio. From mitigating risk to increasing the diversity of your portfolio, there is a lot to gain by trading options. Different people use options for different purposes. Some might use it for diversifying that portfolio, others for earning profits or mitigating risks.

For instance, there's absolutely no reason to believe that the seller incurred a loss if you purchase a call option and earn a profit on it. Just because one person benefits doesn't mean the other one automatically loses. Perhaps the seller managed to mitigate his risk and made more money than you. So, trading in options can never be a zero-sum game.

Profitability Is Associated with Purchasing Either Puts or Calls

An unfortunate concept about trading options is that a trader will be profitable only if they purchase calls or puts. You can earn a profit by executing trades using a single strategy such as purchase or sale. However, this isn't the only way to go about making money. Most strategies commonly used include multiple transactions executed simultaneously, and this is how you can profit. You don't have to stick to selling or purchasing calls alone. Instead, you can write and sell puts or calls, and you can combine all of these. There are plenty of choices out there when it comes to strategy.

Trading in Options Is All about Speculation

When it comes to trading order investment in any form, a little speculation is involved. The same applies to options as well. Trading in options is not just about speculation, but they can also be used to create an additional source of income.

You can also diversify your portfolio and improve your risk tolerance by adding them with other instruments. For instant karma, if you feel the market will be trading within a specific price range, you can decide to trade options by using calendars or condors. There are different strategies that can work wonders, but a lot of planning is required. So, it is unfair to limit options by believing they are solely meant for speculation.

Options Are the Quickest Way to Earn Money Easily

If you want to attain your financial goals or start investing, let go of the notion of a free meal. The concept of a free meal doesn't exist anywhere. If you want something, you need to work for it. Trading might sound simple when looked at superficially, but if you want to be a successful trader, a lot of effort is required. You should not only understand the instrument you are dealing in. Study the market and pay close attention to different events which affect the market and instruments. You need to have sufficient knowledge and experience to become a successful trader. Let go of the notion that trading in options will make you rich overnight. There is always a learning curve, and unless you are willing to learn, you cannot get anywhere.

Options Are Ideal Only for Sellers

A rather befuddling misconception about options trading is that it is ideal only for people who want to sell. Only sellers are believed to be profitable in the options market. This is nothing more than a misconception. If sellers were the only ones who earn a profit, there would never be any options buyers. After all, contracts cannot be executed if no one is interested in purchasing.

An options seller might have a certain advantage over buyers at times. However, all this is subject to change. There are different factors at play here, and at times it's profitable to purchase options instead of selling them.

Whenever you are dealing with options, remember there are multiple ways to attain your financial goals. No strategy is about solely selling or buying. You will learn more about mixed transaction strategies in the subsequent chapters.

Options Will Always Expire Worthlessly

It's entirely up to traders whether they want to exercise their right to buy or sell the underlying security option contracts are based on. The most common practice in an options trade is to close the position before expiry. This applies to almost all different types of options except European options. Options will expire worthlessly at times, and there will be nothing you can do to prevent it.

Some trades are extremely profitable, while others don't do well. This is nothing but a risk every trader takes. However, it is simply untrue that all options expire worthlessly. In fact, there are strategies where traders earn profits if the option expires worthlessly.

Now that you have gone through all these myths, chances are you will feel more confident about trading in options. It is not only interesting to learn but ultimately quite profitable. What matters most at this point is how you go about trading and which options you choose.

Chapter 3: How Are Options Priced?

In the previous chapter, you were familiarized with different terms such as the strike price, market price, premium, time value, intrinsic value, and volatility of options. In this chapter, you will learn more about how each of these influences the pricing of options in the market.

The price a trader pays to purchase an options contract is known as options premium. Three primary factors determine the pricing of an option in the market, and they are:

- Implied volatility

- Intrinsic value

- Time value of an option

Once you understand the difference between each of these, it becomes easier to determine whether any trading decision associated with a specific option is good or bad. After all, the aim of trading in any financial instrument is profitability. Unless you are aware of how much you stand to gain and the cost involved, you cannot make good trades.

Whenever a buyer buys a specific premium for purchasing an option from the option seller, he becomes the option holder. The option seller is the option writer too. Options contracts usually represent 100 shares of an underlying stock of a specific company. The premium payable on options is based on the price per share of this underlying stock. For instance, if the premium payable on a single share is $5, the total cost of the option will be $500. Similarly, if the options contract is valued at $300, it means the premium per share is $3.

The intrinsic value of an option is the difference between the strike price and the existing market value of the underlying security or stock. If the value of the stock of a specific company is trading in the market at $500, the value of the option of such stock is $400.

If a trader has a call option for the said stock at a strike price of $490, it means the intrinsic value of the option is $10. When this happens, the option is said to be in the money. It means that with this specific call option, the investor can earn a profit of $10 per share as per the options contract.

The buyer has the right to purchase an option for $390. Since the market value is $400, he can sell it at the market value and earn a profit of $10. On the other hand, the option will not have any intrinsic value if its market value reduces to $370.

In a case like this, the option is said to be out of the money. If any option is out of the money on its expiry date, it has no value.

Now, let's look at an example for a put option. Once again, let's assume the market price for the stock of a specific company is $400. If an options trader has a put option for said stock with a strike price of $410, its inherent value is $10. Such a put option is said to be in the money.

It gives the buyer a profit of $10 for every share he owns. It means that the trader has a right to purchase an option at $400 and sell it for $410 to earn a profit. If the same trader's put option in the same company has a strike price of only $390, there is no intrinsic value because the market price is higher than the strike price. The put option will be worthless on its expiration and is said to be out of the money in such cases.

An option is said to be more in the money if its intrinsic value is high. There is a direct relationship between the price of an option and the strike price. An option is worthless if it is out of the money on its expiration. If the option expires in the money before the expiry date, it will not have any value due to the implied volatility and time value.

The period during which an option expires is known as its time value. The longer the time frame until expiration, the greater is its time value. Ask the expiry date of an option approach; it's time you start using it. If the option expires, it has no time value. For instance, a trader or holder of an options contract has a stock of a specific company that expires within 30 days. The option he is holding expires at money. Any contract such as this has a higher value when compared to an options contract based on the same underlying stock but with a shorter expiration date. There will be a differentiation in their valuation even when other things stay the same due to the time frame left until its expiration.

The final factor that determines the price of an option is volatility. The volatility of the price of an underlying security, stock, or asset is represented by implied volatility. If the implied volatility of a specific asset is high, it means the value of the underlying security can swing in either direction.

It doesn't matter whether the value of the underlying security increases or decreases. Implied volatility simply shows whether there will be a drastic movement in the value of the underlying stock or not. If the implied volatility of a specific asset is low, it means the chances of extreme price fluctuations are quite low. The higher the price of an option, the higher the level of implied volatility.

Remember all these different factors before you start trading and take them into consideration while calculating the price of an option.

Chapter 4: Strategic Planning

Have you ever established certain goals for yourself, but unfortunately, failed to achieve them? Were you excited and motivated in the beginning, but it did not last for very long? If yes, then it's probably because you did not have a proper plan in place.

Planning and preparation are crucial aspects of life. Regardless of whether it's your personal life or even professional, without planning, you cannot get ahead. If you don't want to become friends with failure, learning to plan efficiently is important. This applies to trading as well.

A trading strategy effectively states what you want to accomplish and how you want to go about doing it. It also states in great detail why you want to accomplish certain goals. Strategic plans review your abilities and skills, improve them, make the most of the resources at your disposal, and help you understand your expectations from trading.

It's not just important to make good trades, but understanding why you want to make them will fuel your motivation to keep going. A strategic plan or a trading strategy serves as a compass to guide you through all the trades you make and to ensure your profitability while minimizing your risk exposure.

If the only thing you try to do is earn greater profits, it opens your portfolio up to greater risks. Unless you learn to shield yourself from these risks, you cannot get ahead.

A good trading strategy gives you valuable insights needed to start outlining all the different steps that need to be taken for evaluating, executing, and managing the investments you make. Before you learn to double up a trading strategy, it's important to answer a few key questions.

- Why do you want to start trading?
- What exactly does success mean to you?
- How do you want to attain your goals?
- Do you have a specific exit strategy in mind?

A trading strategy essentially acts as a skeletal framework for all the traits you decide to make. Having a trading strategy is just one part of the plan. Just because you have created a strategy does not automatically guarantee success. The trading strategy must be effective and realistic for it to be efficient and successful.

A strategy helps in improving your insight into your motivations as well as the goals you have established for trading. How can you develop an iterating strategy, and how does it help with trading? These are the two most common questions most beginners have while talking about strategic planning. In this chapter, you will learn about the benefits of having a trading strategy or a strategic plan before trading and how you can create one.

The Advantages of Having a Trading Strategy

In life, you should always be proactive instead of reactive, and the same applies during investing as well. There is a difference between both these terms if you have never really given it any thought.

Proactive means you have taken an active approach and initiative or lead toward doing something or changing your situation. On the other hand, reactiveness is when you take action after a specific circumstance order situation has occurred. With strategic planning, you become a proactive trader and not just a reactive one.

You cannot control all the events or circumstances that affect the price of financial tools in the trading market. However, you have the power to better manage your finances and ensure you don't suffer massive losses. You have the power to regulate your risk exposure and make the most of the finances available at your disposal.

A good trading strategy helps prepare for different contingencies, reduces risk exposure, and increases the chances of earning better profits.

A trading strategy helps your mind in staying focused. As a trader, you will be exposed to tons of information and data. After going through all this data and information, you need to make decisions.

When you are exposed to such information, it can soon become overwhelming and can also hinder your analysis process. This is where a trading strategy steps into the picture. It helps in understanding and fixing your entry and exit points.

Regardless of how the market performs, how the instruments are doing, or how others feel about trading, you will precisely know when to enter and exit a trade. Instead of blindly following trading fads and trends in the market, you will be making trades based on your financial capacity and sticking to your plan of action.

A good trading strategy helps measure your performance as well. Without measuring your performance, you cannot determine whether you have improved or not. Measuring your performance is also important for making required changes and improving yourself.

Chaotic trading seldom provides any opportunities to assess how you were doing in the market. For instance, after a training period, you might realize you haven't fully utilized all the capital available at your disposal or how you manage your finances. If that's the case, a good trading plan gives you a chance to rectify all this.

This point is in synchronization with the previous one. Strategic planning is important because it helps regulate your emotions. Instead of letting your emotions get the better of you, you learn to control them with a plan.

When you know all the different steps you need to take, entry and exit points in the market and the budget for each trade or the maximum loss you can withstand, making the trades becomes easier. It means, instead of allowing your emotions to guide your decisions, you are using logic and facts.

For instance, if the value of a stock you invested in crashes, the logical action would be to exit the market after cutting all your losses. An emotional decision would be to double down and increase your investment to compensate for the losses, believing the market will turn around.

However, the second solution is riskier than the previous one. If you have a strategy, it becomes easier to stay on the right course and avoid any unrequited deviations. Similarly, there will be instances when it feels like every trade is going your way. In such instances, success can also get to your head.

If you don't have a proper plan in mind, you might end up investing more than you stand to lose, believing in your hot streak.

A good trading plan helps distinguish between good and brilliant ideas. If you have no idea of what you desire to achieve or your reason for the same, anything and everything that pops into your head will seem like a good idea. What do you want to invest in, how much should the investment be, and what are your reasons for this investment?

These are the three questions you will be answering whenever creating a trading plan in order to make better decisions. After all, we all have different wants and needs, but the resources available at our disposal are always finite. Learning to make the most of these resources while working towards your goals or objectives is the key to success.

Over or under trading becomes quite common if a trading plan doesn't describe your entry and exit points. If you don't make the most of the resources available at your disposal or go overboard, you will harm your finances.

Always remember, you should never invest more than you think you can stand to lose in a trade. If you remember these two points, it will become easier for you to make informed decisions while entering the market.

Now that you are aware of all the different benefits associated with establishing a trading plan, it's important to create one. Always remember that it's not just about creating a good trading plan; you should follow it as well.

A plan without any action following it does not amount to anything. Next time whenever you are creating a trading plan, you need to create it such that it fits your needs and requirements.

Forget about everyone else for now. Instead, focus purely on yourself. As long as the plan makes sense to you, it's good. There is no one formula or one size fits all approach when it comes to creating strategic plans for trading.

It is quite personal and will differ from one person to another. Before you start creating a plan, there are some things you should always consider.

- Is there anything specific you want to achieve while trading or investing?

- Do you need a trading plan to get the hang of your finances?

- Do you want to create an additional source of income?

- Do you want to establish a retirement fund or an emergency fund?

- Do you want to secure your child's future?

Are you wondering what all these questions are? These questions will give you better insight into your reasons for trading. You should always have the motivation or an internal desire that pushes you to take action.

Defining what you want to accomplish influences all your financial decisions; once you are aware of this, your internal motivation commands, which is important to understand your risk tolerance. To determine your risk tolerance, here are some simple questions you should answer.

- Would you call yourself a risk taker?

- Are you a conservative investor?

- What is your usual orientation toward risks?

- How do you determine whether the investment decision you're making is good or not?

- Will any other aspect of your life be affected if you assume more risks?

Once you have answered all the questions, you will be aware of your motivations and risk tolerance. Once you are aware of these two aspects, it's important to identify the challenges that stand in your way.

A good trading strategy is seldom complicated and is always effective. Without efficiency, there is no purpose in creating a trading strategy. It doesn't mean you should never use any complex trading techniques. Rather, go about it smartly.

Instead of overwhelming yourself with multiple rules associated with every trade, analyze the techniques you want to use and undo them carefully. The advanced trading strategy is ideal for veterans and not beginners who are just dipping their feet into the waters of options trading. Never forget to factor in your trading requirements and your level of expertise and knowledge before using a specific technique.

Always remember that there is no such thing as a foolproof trading strategy. Regardless of how detailed and well laid out your plans are, certain events and circumstances or happenings will always be out of your control.

All you can do is to ensure that you can adjust yourself to all these changes. The strategy you develop should also be updated from time to time. If not, it will become obsolete. With time, your needs and requirements, investment criteria, and financial objectives will also change. So, the trading strategy should account for all this and accommodate your current requirements.

Depending on the existing conditions in the market, you might have to change or modify a specific trading strategy.

Before you go ahead with a trading strategy, don't forget to test it at least once. This is where demo accounts step into the picture. These days several online platforms offer virtual simulations to test trading strategies. You will learn more about this while selecting a broker.

Before you select a broker or an online trading platform, check for all the resources that it offers, including virtual simulations and demo accounts.

At times, a specific trading strategy might work for some while not for others. This is quite common and should not worry you.

There is no guarantee that the strategy you have chosen will work well for you or not. Even an excellent trading strategy or plan can fail. So, you should always make sure you have a backup. This is one of the reasons why you should never invest more than you can stand to lose.

Always assume the worst and prepare for the best while trading. You will learn more about different trading strategies in the subsequent chapters. For now, let's move on to the next step of creating a trading strategy.

Steps to Follow

Deciding the Market

The first step is to understand the market you wish to invest in. There are different types of underlying assets ranging from stocks to commodities you can invest in while dealing in the options market. So, you must conduct a couple of analyses before you decide on the options you wish to trade with.

First, gather all the financial information available about the specific underlying security you wish to trade with. It helps determine your return on investment, as well as the price to earnings ratio.

Once you do this, it is time to analyze where the investment stands according to the present market trends. It will give you a general idea of a specific asset's performance and how it might perform in the future.

Another analysis you must perform is known as sentiment analysis. It essentially means you need to understand the existing market conditions and the general sentiment of investors towards the market. A bearish or bullish market will influence the kind of trading strategy you opt for.

Select the Direction

Once you have zeroed in on the direction you wish to head in, the next step is to determine the kind of strategy you wish to use. It can be something as simple as a call or a put, or it could be a mix of different strategies to create a strangle or straddle strategy.

Depending on your goals, the existing market conditions, and the kind of investments you wish to make, the strategy will change. Certain strategies are quite good for a bearish market, and some are good for a bullish market. Then are some strategies that can effectively be used when the market is volatile or stagnant. You will learn more about different trading strategies according to the market conditions in the subsequent chapters.

Select an Exit Point

Once you have understood the kind of strategy you wish to use, the next step is to determine your exit points. Determining your exit point is an incredibly important aspect of trading.

It is not only important to determine when you need to jump into the game, but you must also be aware of when you need to exit the game if things don't go as you planned.

For instance, if you decide that your exit point is at 25%, then you must exit the game as soon as your option reaches the specific level, regardless of how well you think it might perform in the future. You must always stick to your trading plan and close a trade as soon as you reach the primary exit point. Apart from a primary exit point, you can also set up a secondary exit point for yourself.

It acts as a buffer and gives your investment a while longer to improve its performance before you need to exit the market. Regardless of the exit point, you wish to set for yourself, ensure that it isn't higher than the financial loss you can risk.

Find well-broken excellence once you have followed all the steps mentioned until now; you must find a good broker or a trading platform to start trading. The options trading markets are such that you always need a third party or a platform to start trading.

While trading, remember to constantly monitor and adjust the investments according to the market and conditions and your preferences. If a strategy doesn't work, don't hesitate to ditch it immediately, you can always look for something else that works.

Depending on the existing conditions and the resources available, do not hesitate to change your strategy as and when needed.

Chapter 5: How to Select a Trading Strategy

Before you start trading in options, it's important to understand why you want to do it. You should also find the right broker, discover different opportunities for trading, and create a trading plan. This is one of the most important steps if you want to make it big as an options trader.

A trading strategy primary signals when you should enter or assume a specific position in the market. Regardless of all the information you have about options, unless you have a proper strategy in place, you cannot make the most of it. A proper strategy helps you make the right decisions to improve your finances and achieve your trading goals.

Perhaps a challenging part of planning a trade is to select the right strategy. This is incredibly important regardless of whether you are a beginner or a veteran in the trading game. The good news is that understanding how to select a trading strategy is quite easy if you take the following aspects into account.

Start With Your Outlook

What you expect from the underlying security you are investing in is known as your outlook. It refers to whether you expect the price of the security to rise or fall in the future. In most types of investing, the only two outlook switches considered to be profitable are believing whether the price will increase or decrease. For instance, stock traders purchase stocks if they believe their value will increase or appreciate.

On the other hand, if they believe the price will fall in the future, they will sell. In stocks, these are the only ways to earn a profit. When it comes to option trading, there are four outlooks that refer to your expectations of how the market will perform. The market can be bullish, bearish, neutral, or volatile.

If your outlook is bullish, it means you expect the price of the underlying security to increase. If you believe the price will decrease, you have a bearish outlook.

If you believe the price will stay relatively the same, it's a neutral outlook. A volatile outlook is when you believe the price will sway in either direction, or this movement will be significant. It becomes easier to find the right strategy to trade with when you select your outlook.

For instance, if you believe the price of the underlying security will show a significant appreciation, the strategy you opt for wouldn't generate profits based on small movements of security in the market. At times, traders expect the price of an underlying security to stay relatively neutral for the time being and significantly increase in the future.

You can always combine the outlooks and change them according to your general style or perspective.

Consider the Risk

You cannot overlook the risk involved in trading. There is no such thing as a 100% safe trade. Of course, certain strategies can be used to reduce this risk, while others are extremely risky.

Your approach should be based on your risk profile. As a rule of thumb, it is common to never invest more than you can stand to lose. For instance, if you can only lose $10, it doesn't make any sense to invest $20. Let go of the notion that trading in options is a way to get rich overnight.

Always consider the risk to reward ratio as well. Usually, it's believed that the reward is directly proportional to the risk involved. It means the higher the risk, the greater the reward. So, calculate the total risk you can sustain without causing any significant dents in your finances.

Selecting a strategy becomes easier when you know how much you stand to lose. This is a cardinal rule of investing in any security or instrument. Never overlook it because, if you are not careful, you might end up neck-deep in debt.

Using Spreads

Creating spreads is an important part of options trading. You will primarily be combining multiple positions to enter and exit the market. When you use spreads, it becomes easier to mitigate the risk associated with your investment options, and it also reduces the cost of investment.

Using spreads is believed to be a better trading option than holding onto a single position. When you enter a single trade or position, you are investing in only a specific type of options contract.

It reduces the number of transactions involved, but the commission you will end up paying on each day will be higher. Initially, it's better to stick with single positions until you get the hang of it. Once you understand the ropes of options trading, you can use spreads.

Don't worry, the different strategies outlined in the next chapters will guide you through all this.

Number of Trades

Creating a trading account with a reputed broker is important if you want to become a serious options trader. Most trading accounts have specific limits set in place to protect the interest of the customers. It means they prevent you from assuming greater risk than you can withstand.

The trading limits are also set and placed for start and regulatory purposes. Depending on the trading level associated with your brokerage account, the amount you stand to invest also depends on this. It is an important consideration when selecting a trading strategy.

The Complexity of the Strategy

There will always be strategies of varying degrees of complexity. Certain strategies are a combination of multiple consecutive transactions, while others involve only one or two.

Depending on your level of understanding, common knowledge, comfort level, and risk, the complexity of the strategy you opt for will also differ.

Your entry and exit points in the market essentially determine whether you stand to earn a profit or anchor or loss.

The complexity increases if there are multiple transactions and underlying securities or assets. As you start going through all the different strategies discussed in the following chapters, you will understand that some transactions are easy to make while others take a little getting used to.

As with anything in life, a lot of practice is needed until you can improve your ability as an options trader. Once you have sufficient knowledge and confidence, executing complicated strategies becomes easier.

Chapter 6: Trading Strategies for Beginners

In the previous chapter, we mentioned that there are four primary outlooks in options trading. Unless you decide upon a specific one, you cannot select a strategy you want to use. In this chapter, let's look at the different trading outlooks in detail to get a better understanding of the one that suits you.

Bearish Outlook

Traders are believed to have a bearish outlook when they believe the price of the underlying security will diminish. Bears in the market earn a profit only by purchasing put options. The option expires worthless if there is no change in the underlying securities price.

If you believe there is going to be a smaller drop in the price of the underlying asset, investing in put options is not desirable.

If you want to take a position based on a downward trend in the price of an underlying asset but don't want to risk most of the capital involved, investing in putting options and writing puts reduces the risk through cost payable upfront. To reduce the time decay on the investment made, consider writing some calls.

The most common strategies applicable to a bearish market are:

- Long Put
- Short Call
- Bear Put Spread
- Bear Call Spread
- Bear Ratio Spread
- Short Bear Ratio Spread
- Bear Butterfly Spread
- Bear Put Ladder Spread

Bullish Outlook

Unlike bears, bullish traders believe the price of the underlying security or asset will see a positive movement. A bullish outlook is one of the most common outlooks in the market.

While using any bullish strategy, the obvious way to earn a profit is by investing in calls based on the notion that the price of the underlying security will increase in the future.

If price movement in the market isn't much or is moderate, it is not the right strategy. If there is any decrease in the price of the underlying security, you will incur a loss.

Investing in calls is a trading strategy on its own. In several circumstances, purchasing calls can be quite profitable. At the same time, there are certain disadvantages too.

You will lose the entire investment if the option expires worthless, and this is a risk associated with all bullish strategies. With a bullish outlook, please beware of the negative consequences associated with time decay. You will profit only when the price of the underlying security is significant. That said, buying calls is never a bad idea.

You can always use a trading strategy to reduce the cost involved to purchase calls by simultaneously writing calls with a higher strike price.

It reduces the effect of time decay on the position you are assuming in the market. While using bullish strategies, you can create credit spreads to reduce the upfront costs associated with a debit spread.

A wonderful thing about using bullish strategies is it lets you assume a position that profits from any increase in the underlying assets price. Apart from this, you can also control different factors associated with an investment, like the capital needed and the risk involved.

If you want to make a quick buck, be aware of the sacrifice involved. This applies to all trading strategies in the options market. The main drawback of using a bullish trading strategy is that the profit you earn will be limited to a specific amount. Since most of the trades in the options markets are based on relatively short-term movements and prices, it is not a major drawback. Holding onto a trade for longer periods means your ability to hold multiple positions should be sustainable.

The most common strategies applicable to a bullish market are:

- Long Call
- Short Put
- Bull Call Spread
- Bull Put Spread
- Bull Ratio Spread
- Short Bull Spread
- Bull Butterfly Spread
- Bull Condor Spread
- Bull Call Ladder Spread

Neutral Outlook

If the financial tools in the market don't show any changes in price, they are known as neutral. Although this is a general definition, the term has a broader meaning in options trading. If the price of the underlying securities moves with an effect arranged or stays the same, the investor earns a profit; the first of these is known as neutral trading strategies. If there is a slight up or down movement in the price of an underlying security, it's believed to be moving sideways. When the price starts moving sideways, the security is projecting a neutral trend.

The very existence of these strategies is the obvious advantage they offer. It doesn't necessarily mean the price of the securities keeps changing in the market. Depending on different conditions, the market reacts differently.

If the price of underlying assets is relatively stable, you still stand to gain a profit. It means you don't have to have a bearish or bullish outlook; you can benefit from a neutral trend as well.

A trade-off from these trends, when the price of security doesn't move, is that there is only a minor price change in either direction. If any of these outcomes occur, you earn a profit. These trading strategies give you better control over managing and mitigating your portfolio's risk.

The most common trading strategies applicable to a neutral market are:

- Covered Call

- Covered Put

- Covered Call Collar
- Short Straddle
- Short Gut
- Calendar Call Spread
- Call Ratio Spread
- Calendar Put Spread
- Put Ratio Spread
- Calendar Straddle
- Calendar Strangle
- Butterfly Spread
- Condor Spread
- Short Iron Butterfly Spread
- Iron Condor Spread
- Iron Albatross Spread

Volatile Outlook

In a volatile market, you will earn profits when the prices of an underlying security show some volatility. A financial tool is volatile when it shows a significant price movement in either direction. That said, you cannot always determine in which direction the price will move.

For instance, the volatility of a company stock will increase if there are rumors of takeovers or mergers. These are also known as dual directional trading strategies.

It means you stand to profit regardless of whichever direction the price moves in. For instance, you can invest in an equal number of calls and put options of the same security at a specific strike price. So, you will earn a profit, regardless of the direction the price decides to move.

On the downside, you cannot use these strategies unless there is obvious volatility in the market. If the price movement is insignificant or close to staying neutral, you cannot apply these strategies.

The most common strategies applicable to a volatile market are:

- Long Straddle
- Long Strangle
- Strip Straddle
- Strip Strangle
- Strap Strangle
- Strap Straddle

- Long Gut
- Call Ratio Backspread
- Put Ratio Backspread
- Short Calendar Call Spread
- Short Calendar Put Spread
- Short Butterfly Spread
- Short Condor Spread
- Reverse Iron Butterfly Spread
- Reverse Iron Condor Spread

Don't be overwhelmed by looking at all the different strategies involved in options trading. Once you get the hang of it, executing these strategies and holding different positions in the market becomes easier.

Remember to keep practicing whatever you learn to improve your skills as an options trader. You will learn about each of these strategies in detail in the next chapters.

Chapter 7: Strategies for Bears

Bearish traders have a pessimistic outlook toward the market. They believe the financial tool's value will experience a downward swing, and they try to profit from the decline in the market value.

It means bears are essentially sellers. If you have a bearish outlook toward the market, here are the different strategies you can use.

Long Put

This is one of the most straightforward bearish trading strategies. You simply need to purchase put options off an underlying security or asset. The expiry date of the option, the strike price of the contract, and opting for an American or European option are the three considerations when using this strategy.

The upfront cost payable for acquiring the put options and the potential profit you can earn are influenced by the strike price of the contract. If you are just getting started with options trading, opt for at-the-money contracts. With these, the current trading price and the strike price are always the same for an underlying security.

You can also select out of the money or in the money contracts as well, depending on your preferences. As compared to in the money options, out of the money options are relatively cheaper.

If the value of the underlying security reduces, you will earn a profit in the long put. The greater the price reduction, the higher is your profitability. You can earn a profit by using a long put in different circumstances.

The first is to use a sell order to close your position. Alternatively, you can purchase the underlying security and later sell it at the strike price. That said, you would lose your investment if the price of underlying security doesn't go below the strike price of the options you own.

While using this contract, the maximum loss you can incur is equivalent to the money spent acquiring the contracts before the trade was made.

Short Call

While using a short call, you are selling a call option that comes with an obligation of purchasing the underlying security or asset at an agreed price sometime in the future. The profit on potential is limited if the stock is trading in the market less than the strike price at which it was sold.

The risk increases if the price of the stock is more than the strike price. If you believe the value of the underlying asset will show a moderate decline, use a short call. The time decay factor plays in your favor while using the strategy, and you can benefit even if the price of the underlying asset stays relatively stable.

Bear Put Spread

To execute a bear put spread, two simultaneous transactions need to be made in the market. The first transaction is to purchase money puts.

The next transaction is to execute an equal number of monies put for a contract with a lower strike price than the previous trade. While executing this spread, ensure the contracts are both for the same underlying security. The contracts should also have the same expiry date.

Bear Call Spread

At times, the value of an underlying security might reduce, but the decline is steep. In these cases, a bear call spread comes in handy. If there is a moderate reduction in the value of the underlying security, you can still earn a profit.

You need to execute two simultaneous contracts while using this strategy. Purchase and sell a fixed number of calls with the same underlying security or asset expiring on the same date. The only point of difference is the strike price of options contracts. You need to purchase out of the money call options while selling at-the-money call options.

Remember, the date of expiry and the underlying asset must be the same.

Bear Ratio Spread

This is quite similar to the usual bear put spread. The only difference is in a bed ratio spread; the number of options contracts you will be writing and purchasing are different.

Even if the value of the underlying security doesn't decrease drastically or it increases slightly, you can still use this bearish strategy due to the spread involved. You need to execute three simultaneous transactions to execute the strategy.

The first one is to purchase money put at a higher strike price while executing other money puts at a lower strike price. Even if the value of the underlying security doesn't increase or decrease significantly, the only loss is the upfront investment of procuring the contracts.

If the value of the underlying security on the date of expiry is the same as the strike price of at-the-money puts, the trade is said to be profitable.

Short Bear Ratio Spread

This trading strategy is an advanced version of the long-put trading strategy discussed previously. If you firmly believe that the price of the underlying security will experience a drastic reduction and you are interested in reducing the upfront costs involved in procuring the options contract, you still strategize.

As with any other options spread strategy, be prepared to enter simultaneous positions to use and execute the strategy. You need to enter the two contracts simultaneously, which are based on the same underlying security with the same date of expiry.

However, there are two other considerations while executing such trades. The first is to remember that you need to have a higher strike price than the ones you are purchasing. The number of contracts you want to sell needs to be lower than the contracts you purchase.

If you are comfortable with executing multiple contracts simultaneously, you can enter into three positions. Whenever you are entering any credit, remember the two conditions discussed here. Your ability to earn a profit is directly proportional to the ratio within the spread created.

Bear Butterfly Spread

If you think the value of an underlying security will decrease within a specific timeframe, a bear butterfly spread comes in handy. Once again, you can reduce the option and cost of investment while using this strategy. If your capital available for investment is low, use those. That said, your profitability is also relatively low.

You need to execute three transactions simultaneously to create a bear butterfly spread. Before the execution of these transactions, select a specific price range in which you believe the underlying security will dimension value. Apart from this, you also need to select a timeframe within which this decline will happen. Once you do these right, put contracts with a strike price equivalent to the price and expiry date as per your prediction.

For every two puts written by you, purchase one put with a higher strike price and another with a lower strike price.

Remember, all these options contracts need to expire on the same day. The strike price for all the different options contracts you have purchased and executed should not be spread wide apart and need to be close together if you want a profit.

Bear Put Ladder Spread

The bear put ladder spread is an advanced version of the regular bear put spread strategy discussed previously. As with any other bearish outlook strategy, your profitability increases as the value of the underlying asset falls.

Once again, you need to execute multiple options contracts at the same time. As with any other spread strategy, this reduces the upfront costs involved in procuring and executing the contract. There are three different transactions you need to execute.

This is perhaps one of the most complicated bearish strategies.

The first options contract is to purchase put options with the idea of earning a profit if the value of an underlying security diminishes as per your predictions.

The other two transactions you need to perform are writing two contracts for an equal number of put options. While doing this, ensure one contract of put options has a lower strike price than the other.

Whenever you are executing a bear put ladder spread, insured go options are always at the money or relatively close to the money when you purchase them.

One contract of options you write should be such that its strike price is equivalent to the expected decline in the value of the underlying security. In the final set of puts, you need to have a lower strike price than the ones you have executed.

This brings us to the end of all the different strategies applicable to a bearish market. If you believe the price of an underlying security will reduce or the market is in a downward spiral, use any of these.

Start with the relatively simple ones and get the hang of executing one contract at a time. After this, you can move on to the relatively advanced strategies.

Chapter 8: Strategies for Bulls

Unlike bears, bulls have a rather optimistic outlook about the market and how it will move. Instead of believing the market will decline, bullish traders believe though the market value will appreciate.

They are investing based on the notion that the market conditions will improve, and the securities will perform better. In this chapter, we will look at some common bullish trading strategies applicable to the options market.

Long Call

A long call comes in handy if you believe the value of an underlying security will increase significantly within a relatively short period. Even if the price movement of the underlying asset isn't steep or quick, you still stand to earn a profit. There is only one factor you need to remember while executing the strategy - the negative effect of time decay on the value of the underlying security.

The value of the asset reduces if the expiration date of the call is approaching. The risk of your portfolio is limited to the cost incurred for acquiring the calls contracts. You will profit by using the strategy as long as the price of the underlying asset increases. You have two options here: filter out the first asset to sell the calls when there is an increase in the price of an underlying asset.

The second option is to purchase an underlying asset or security at a predetermined strike price and later sell it at the current trading price in the market. You can use either of these strategies while executing a long call to earn a profit.

Short Put

As the name suggests, you will be selling put options in this strategy. In this, you agree to procure underlying securities at a predetermined price and date. If the value of the underlying security increases, you profit from this strategy. If the value decreases, the puts you have written need to be executed.

If that's the case, you will essentially be purchasing underlying securities from the options contracts. Use this option only if you are certain that the value of the underlying security will increase.

To execute the strategy right, put options that are close to the money and have a short expiry date. When you execute such a contract, you don't have to worry about any drastic movement in the value of the underlying security because the timeframe is limited.

Bull Call Spread

This is one of the most commonly used bullish trading strategies. You need to execute options contracts simultaneously. As a bullish trader, you expect the value of an underlying asset to increase. However, there will be instances where the movement isn't drastic. If the movement is drastic, with a regular long call, you cannot earn much of a profit. In such instances, bull call spread comes in handy. The first transaction was to purchase out of the money calls. The second transaction is to write an equal number of add the money calls.

Both these contracts should be based on the same underlying asset. When you do this, a debit spread is created, which reduces the overall cost of writing and buying the calls. The strike price of both contracts you are executing should be placed close together. If the value of the underlying security increases, the trade will be profitable.

Bull Put Spread

To use this strategy, you must execute two put options- long and short put. The long put should have a relatively high strike price when compared to the short put. The expiry date for both of these options contracts must be the same.

And this strategy comes in handy whenever you believe the underlying security will experience a moderate increase in its price, or its overall value will stay stable shortly. To build a bull put spread, you must sell and purchase and add the money put options based on the same underlying security expiring on the same day.

Bull Ratio Spread

This strategy takes our regular bull call spread a step further. The flexibility offered by this trading strategy is greater when compared to a regular bull call spread. You need to execute three options contracts simultaneously. You must purchase two calls while writing one call with a higher strike price than the ones purchased.

It is known as a ratio spread because you are essentially purchasing underwriting calls in a fixed ratio. As a rule of thumb, a usual ratio spread is executed in the ratio of 1:2. It means that for every call option purchased at the money, two out of the money call options need to be written. This ratio can be changed according to your investment objective and the capital available.

Short Bull Spread

You will earn a profit by investing in such securities whose value appreciates similarly to how it would if you were purchasing call options. The cost involved in performing the transactions is reduced while your profitability increases with the strategy.

Be prepared to execute two simultaneous transactions. The first transaction is to purchase calls, and the second is to write calls. To purchase calls, give the broker an open-to-buy order and issue a sell to open order to write the calls. Remember, no contracts should expire on the same date and must be based on the same underlying security. The number of options contracts purchased must be greater than the ones that are written. The usual ratio used in a short bull spread is 3:1. It means that for every 3-call option purchased, you need to write one.

Bull Butterfly Spread

This is quite similar to a regular butterfly spread. The only difference is that the outlook of the trader is not neutral and is instead bullish. Whenever the trader expects the value of an underlying security to appreciate and has a general idea of the limit, which will increase within a fixed period, the strategy is used.

You can still use the strategy with limited capital because the upfront costs involved to make the required transactions are relatively low. Three simultaneous transactions need to be executed to create a bull butterfly spread.

You need to execute a call option with a strike price equivalent to the expected value of an underlying security at a specific date or its expiration. For every two calls that are written, purchase one call with the next lowest possible strike price and one with the next highest strike price.

Once again, these are all assumptions. The money received from writing the calls covers the cost of procuring the calls. On the expiry date, if the value of an underlying asset is the same as the strike price for all the calls written, it is a profitable trade. All the calls that were written will be worthless upon expiration, and all the calls purchased will have a higher strike price earning you a profit. However, all the calls that were purchased at a lower strike price will expire at money.

Bull Condor Spread

You earn a profit by using a bill Condor spread if the value of an underlying security appreciates within the price range you predicted. It's similar to a butterfly spread, but the level of accuracy isn't as high as a butterfly spread.

You need to execute four simultaneous transactions while using the strategy. You need to purchase the right options contracts. All these contracts should be executed at once to reduce the upfront costs involved and to keep things simple. Start by deciding a specific price range if you believe the underlying asset will appreciate within a given timeframe.

The best way to understand the strategy is through an example. Let's assume the stock of a company is trading at $10, and you believe its price will increase between the range of $11-14. The four transactions you will execute involve purchasing and writing calls.

Write calls for the strike price of $11 and execute a similar number of calls with a strike price of $14. Now, purchase call options with a strike price of $6 and $18 each. You are essentially writing a set of calls such that one will be towards the higher end of the predicted price range while the other would be towards the lower end. You are also purchasing two sets of called options, one with a lower and the other with a relatively higher strike price.

While doing this, all the options contracts should be based on the same underlying security expiring on the same date. If the price range you predicted is close together and the contracts are executed within this range, you will be profitable.

Bull Call Ladder Spread

This strategy is an advanced version of a usual bull call spread you were introduced to earlier. If you are confident the value of an underlying security will increase but aren't fully sure if it will increase by significant value or not, use this strategy.

You need to execute three options contracts while implementing the strategy. Purchase calls on the expected value of the underlying security you believe will increase. Now, it's time to write two different sets of calls with varying strike prices.

Here is a simple example to make things clear. Let's assume the stock of a company is currently trading at $80 in the market. You believe its value will increase to $90 and will not exceed this range.

The first transaction is to purchase calls at money at the strike price of $80, while the second transaction has to write the same number of calls for a strike price of $90. You execute the 3rd transaction by writing another set of options for a strike price of $92. By executing all these transactions simultaneously, the costs incurred from the first one will be offset by the money obtained from the other two transactions.

By doing this, you are automatically reducing the upfront costs of executing the trades. If the value of the underlying security moves according to your predicted price range, your trade is profitable.

Chapter 9: Trading in a Neutral Market

The market does not always need to be bullish or bearish, as there will be instances when everything seems neutral. If that's the case or if you have a neutral perspective towards the market, here are some strategies that will come in handy.

Covered Call

This is an incredibly simple strategy and is perfect for beginners. It is a combination of simultaneous purchase of stock and sale of a call options. You can use this strategy if you want to earn from the investment or wish to hold onto the chosen stocks.

Don't exercise the call option until the value of an underlying asset is greater than its strike price, while the call options will be sold out of the money. You are creating a trade-off of priorities by using a covered call.

Covered Put

By using this strategy, you will earn a profit from an underlying stock that is short sold and whose price has not declined any further. Whenever a trader believes the value of stock or shares will reduce, it is short sold.

You need to write a sufficient number of put options to cover the value of the stock you have short sold. Those two decisions need to be made while using a covered put. Both are associated with the strike price of both put options and their expiration date.

As a general rule of thumb, write contracts are at-the-money or just out of money to establish the strike price. You can also select a lower strike price. However, if you do this, the profits you stand to gain will be lower.

Covered Call Collar

The best time to use this strategy is if you already own stock. Two transactions are involved in creating this collar spread. Start by writing calls on the stock you own and then purchase the same number of put options. Both these transactions must expire on the same date. Select a longer expiration window if you believe the value of the stock seems stable in the foreseeable future.

The out of the money calls transacted must be higher in value than the current price of the stock in your possession. This trade will be profitable only if the value of the stock is the same as the strike price of calls executed.

Short Straddle

If the value of an underlying security does not undergo any drastic changes, you can use a short straddle strategy to earn a decent profit. Remember, your trade will only be profitable if the value of a specific security is within a predefined trading range. You need to write at-the-money call options coupled with add the money put options. Your expectation as a trader is to earn a return based on the value of the underlying security.

The assumption is this value will stay stable or will not show any drastic changes. While executing the call and put options, ensure their expiry date is the same.

Short Gut

You can use this strategy if you believe the value of an underlying security will stay within a predefined limit for a specific period. It is quite similar to a short straddle strategy in a way. The only difference is that the price range it offers is rather wide when compared to the previous one.

While using a short gut, you must execute in the money call options for a specific underlying security. Once you do this, you need to simultaneously execute an equal number of in the money call options on the same security. The expiry date of the contracts will be the same. It is entirely up to you to decide whether you want to opt for a short-term or long-term expiry date.

If it is a short-term date, the chances of any drastic price movements in the value of the underlying security reduce. The extrinsic value of short-term options is less when compared to long-term ones.

While using this strategy, you will earn a profit only if the extrinsic value of the option reduces. The lower the extrinsic value, the lower your profitability. The calls and puts executed need to be both in the money. The strike prices must be selected in a way that they are equidistant from the existing trading price of the underlying security.

Here is a simple example to understand how a short gut strategy is executed. Let's assume the current trading price for the stock of a company is $20. You believe the price will stay close to $20.

In the money call options for the stock, it has a strike price of $15 and is trading at $6. Now, you need to write one contract of 100 options that will cost you $600. For in the money put options, the strike price is $25, and they are also currently trading at $6 each.

So, you need to execute another contract of 100 in the money put options for a credit of $600. If you do this, you manage to create a short gut for a total cost of $1200 payable upfront. If the stock price stays at $20, you earn a return of $200 on this investment.

Short Strangle

This is quite similar to a short straddle strategy. You need to execute options on the assumption they will expire out-of-money to make a profitable trade. The relationship between the price and the losses while making this trade is directly proportional. Any significant movement in the price of underlying security increases the scope of a loss. Generally, it's better to select a shorter expiry period to increase your profitability.

The chances of extreme or drastic price movements increase if the timeframe increases. If this happens, you will incur a significant loss. You need to write out of the money options and execute a trade.

While doing this, you need to decide how far out of the money the options will be on the expiry date. You need to execute two contracts here, the first one is a short call with a high strike price, and the next one is a short put with a lower strike price.

Calendar Call Spread

To use a calendar call spread, you need to execute two different trades. You must execute calls on underlying security with a near-term expiration. Once you execute this, you must purchase an equal number of calls on the same underlying security at the same strike price.

The only difference is the expiry date in the second contract will be longer. The profits earned will be the result of time decay on the value of options you have purchased. When compared to a long-term option, a short-term or near-term option loses its value at a quicker rate.

Call Ratio Spread

To execute this strategy, you must purchase options at a lower strike price. After executing this trade, you need to sell all higher numbers of options at a higher strike price. Remember, these contracts must be executed on the same underlying security.

If you believe the price of an underlying asset will increase moderately in the near future, you should use this strategy. To execute the strategy, you need to purchase in the money or add the money call options while selling another out of the money call options.

The expiry date and underlying security will once again stay the same. If the strike price of the options increases on their expiry, you will earn a profit.

Calendar Put Spread

To use a calendar put strategy, there are two steps you must follow. The first is to write put options on the underlying security. These options are written with the notion that the price of the underlying security will stay stable. The expiry date of the output options must be near term.

Usually, it's less than a month. The second step is to purchase an equal number of options on the same underlying security with the same strike price but with a later expiry date.

In a way, it's quite similar to the calendar spread, but the only difference is instead of using calls, you will be creating a spread using put options.

Put Ratio Spread

This is a relatively complex strategy, but the results that it offers are significant. You stand to earn a profit if the value of an underlying security doesn't change.

At the same time, it offers a double benefit of earning a return even if the price of the security increases regardless of how much the price changes as long as there is a price change. You need to execute the contract simultaneously.

You need to buy the right put options as it creates a credit spread to improve your profitability.

If the value of an underlying security is the same as the strike price of the options you have written on their expiry, your profits are maximized while using the strategy. You need to purchase options at a higher strike price and sell more options on the same security at a lower strike price.

If you believe the value of the underlying assets will readily be used, but this decline is only moderate, use the strategy. It also reduces the upfront costs involved because both the trades are executed simultaneously.

Calendar Straddle

The strategy is a perfect mix of call and put option contracts that will be executed simultaneously. It is the combination of two strategies that were covered earlier- short straddle and long straddle. So, you need to execute transactions while using the strategy. Start by writing at-the-money calls with a short-term expiry date and right at-the-money puts for the same expiry date.

After these two contracts, you need to purchase calls and puts, which are both in the money, but with a later expiry date. The profitability of this strategy depends on the effect of time decay. Due to the differences in their expiry dates, it gives you a chance to earn a significant return.

Calendar Strangle

You must execute four transactions while using the strategy. Before using a calendar struggle, you must have a thorough understanding of short strangle and long strangle. You need to buy and write calls. The first step is to write out of the money call options with a near-term expiration along with out of the money puts with the same near-term expiry date.

Now, you must purchase out of the money calls and out of the money puts with a later date of expiration.

The contracts you purchase will be of higher value when compared to the ones you write to the additional time value included. The strike price for the calls you write and the ones you purchase must be the same. Opt for a strike price such that it is just out of the money.

The puts you have written and purchased must also have the same strike price, which is equivalent to the money you have spent purchasing them. If the value of the underlying asset is relatively stable, the calls which have a near-time expiry will expire worthlessly.

However, the other two calls and puts you have executed will still hold value due to the effect of time decay.

Butterfly Spread

Three transactions must be simultaneously executed to use butterfly spread. Start by purchasing in the money calls and the same number of out of the money calls. While you do this, you should also execute twice the number of at-the-money call options.

The underlying asset and the expiry date for all these contracts will be the same. The expiration timeframe is controlled by you, and you can keep it short or long-term, according to your requirements. Setting a closer expiry date is always a better idea.

The strike prices for the in the money and out of the money options must be equal distance from their existing trading price of the underlying security in the market. If the strike price is closer to the existing trading price, your profitability reduces. If the strike price is further apart from the existing prices in the market, your upfront costs increase.

Short Iron Butterfly Spread

If you believe there will be no movement or little movement in the price of an underlying security, you can use this strategy. The aim is to try and accurately predict the value of the stock on its expiry date.

Your profitability in this strategy is determined by the time value of the contracts executed. This is a combination of bull call and puts spreads. You need to purchase one at-the-money call option while buying another out of the money put option.

Once again, it's important to remember the option contracts are based on the same underlying security. All these options should also expire on the same date.

Iron Albatross Spread

An iron albatross spread is believed to be one of the most complicated strategies you can use while trading options. In this strategy, four simultaneous contracts are executed.

These transactions are a combination of writing and buying put and call options. You need to purchase and write out of the money call and put options. The next set of transactions will be to purchase and sell out of the money call options. While doing this, the strike price of the call options you are selling must be higher than the call options you are buying.

Similarly, the strike price of the put options you decide to sell should be lower than the ones you are purchasing. This difference in buying price and strike prices influences your level of profitability.

Condor Spread

This strategy is quite similar to an albatross spread. The primary difference between them is the strike price of the options contracts executed in the albatross spread are further apart when compared to the ones in a Condor spread.

You cannot make a profitable trade unless the strike price of the options contracts executed is set close together. The call and put options executed in all the transactions should be for the same security with the same expiry date. The strike prices should be such that they are equidistant from the existing market price of the underlying asset.

Chapter 10: Trading in a Volatile Market

At times, the general conditions in the market can be quite volatile. It essentially means the price of different securities can swing in either direction. You might not know if the price will increase or decrease, but you do know there will be a significant change in its value. In such situations, here are all the different strategies that can be used.

Long Straddle

This strategy is a combination of long put and long call strategies. You need to purchase at-the-money call options and execute at-the-money put options for the same amount.

Both these transactions are executed simultaneously and have the same expiry date. Since it is a long-term strategy, you have sufficient time to earn a profit due to any price movements in the value of an underlying asset. The scope for profitability from any changes in the value of an underlying asset is rather low if the option has a short-term expiry date.

Your profitability increases because of the time value associated with the call and put options that you will be executing.

Long Strangle

This strategy is also known as strangle strategy. You need to execute multiple transactions simultaneously. The first set of transaction is to purchase calls on an underlying security.

Once you have these end players execute the same number of put options for the same security, the options contracts you are executing must always be out of the money and should be executed simultaneously.

Instead of opting for options that are far out of the money, it is always better to opt for ones that are just out of the money. Ensure that the strike price for the set of transactions is equal distance from the existing trading value.

Strip Straddle

This is quite similar to a long straddle strategy that was discussed above. You must purchase at-the-money call options and at-the-money put options. The primary difference is the number of call options to purchase will be lower than the put options.

The underlying asset and date of expiry for both these transactions are the same. Your profitability is determined by the ratio of put and call options executed. As a rule of thumb, it's always better to purchase at least two put options for every call option executed.

Strip Strangle

While using this strategy, your profitability is directly associated with any drastic changes in the price of an underlying asset in either direction. The profitability increases if the price of underlying security declines instead of following an upward curve.

Options contracts should be executed such that you are purchasing out of the money calls and out of the money puts. Ensure the total number of put options is higher than the call options.

As a rule of thumb, it's always better to execute one out of the money call option for every two out of the money put option contracts.

Strap Strangle

This strategy is similar to a long strangle strategy. Don't use it unless you're confident there will be a drastic movement in the value of an underlying security in the market. The profit of the price of the underlying asset follows an upward trajectory. You need to execute multiple contracts simultaneously to create a strap strangle.

Purchase out of the money put options and out of the money call options. Once again, though, the number of call options executed must be higher than the put options. You need to purchase twice as many out of the money calls as puts. The call to put ratio is 2:1.

Strap Straddle

This strategy shares certain similarities with the long straddle strategy. You need to purchase at-the-money calls and at-the-money put options for the same underlying security expiring on the same date.

The number of calls purchased must be greater than the puts executive. The basic ratio you will be using is 2:1 once again. If you are certain the value of an underlying asset is following an upward trend, use the strategy.

Long Gut Next line: To execute this strategy, purchase call options that are in the money. You need to purchase the same number of in the money put options as well.

Ping all the option contracts to be executed on the same underlying security with the same date of expiration. The strike price along with the expiry date are the primary factors influencing your profitability while using the strategy.

To reduce the upfront costs in the world, the strike prices of the call and put options should be relatively close to their current trading price in the market.

Call Ratio Backspread

Even though the call ratio back spread is a volatile trading strategy, it has bullish features. You earn a profit only if there is an upward movement in the value of the underlying asset. If there is no upward swing, your profitability reduces. You need to execute two transactions to create this spread. You need to purchase the right call options.

It is an array or a spread, and therefore the total number of options executed in each of these transactions is not the same. Purchase calls for every call that's written. The total credit for all the contracts executed must always be higher than the debit on the ones purchased.

A primary benefit of using this strategy is it limits your losses. So, it becomes easier to calculate your overall risk exposure.

Put Ratio Backspread

Even though this is a volatile options trading strategy, it has bearish features. The reason why this strategy is believed to be bearish is that profitability increases if the value of the underlying security reduces or shows a downward trend and starts an upward one.

You stand to incur losses if there is no change in the price of an underlying security or the change is minimal. You need to purchase the right put options. Both these transactions are for the same underlying security with the same expiry date.

You need to purchase an equal number of calls and put options. Through call options, you must be in the money while the put options are at the money.

Short Calendar Call Spread

If you want to use this spread, it doesn't matter which direction the price of the underlying asset moves as long as there is a drastic movement. By using the strategy comment, you can capitalize on price movement in either direction.

Use the strategy only after you master all the other strategies discussed until now. To create a short calendar spread, two transactions need to be executed simultaneously. The first transaction is to purchase at-the-money call options. The second is to write about the money call options.

You are purchasing and writing call options simultaneously. Because it is a calendar spread, the expiry date of both these contracts will be different. Profitability is based on the time decay of options contracts executed.

It is also a credit spread, and therefore, there are hardly any upfront costs payable for creating the strategy. That said, you should also maintain a specific margin in your trading account to use it.

Short Calendar Put Spread

A short put calendar spread helps on a profit using the time decay of contracts executed. Two simultaneous transactions need to be executed using this volatile market strategy.

Start by purchasing out of the money put options while simultaneously writing at-the-money puts. Out of the money put options are relatively cheaper to acquire and offer a higher net credit.

This automatically increases your profitability. However, if the value of the underlying security or asset decreases, the price of the options return will be higher than the one acquired.

It, in turn, increases the risk of loss. The date of expiry and underlying asset for both these options contracts is the same. The value of the contract with a longer expiry date will be higher than the ones with a shorter expiration.

It is primarily based on the idea that any movement in the value of an underlying asset, as long as it's a substantial movement, will ensure that the extrinsic value of body option contracts will be closed or equal to being full.

Short Butterfly Spread

This strategy is based on the simultaneous execution of three options contracts and transactions. Now, it is entirely up to you whether you want to execute the contract based on put or call options. To improve your understanding of the strategy, here's a simple example using call options.

The first transaction executed is to sell in the money calls. The second step is to execute the same number of out of the money call options. The final transaction is to purchase twice as many money calls as the calls you have written.

The expiry date will be different for all these transactions. Ideally, for beginners, it is suggested you should stick with the same expiry date. The only decision you are left with is to decide the strike price.

The simplest way to establish the strike prices is by selecting one that is equidistant from the existing value of the underlying security.

All in the money calls executed need to be in the money, while all the out of the money options you have written must be as out of the money as possible. This is the only way to improve your profitability while using the strategy.

Short Condor Spread

While using this strategy, you have absolute control over deciding the strike price of the options executed for optimizing your preferences and profitability. There are four simultaneous transactions you need to execute for creating this spread.

Once again, you have the option of choosing either call or put transactions. Here is a simple example using call transactions to give you a better idea of how a short corner spread is created.

The primary idea is regardless of whether it's a call or a put option you are executing, pay attention to the strike prices.

The first transaction is to execute a call option that is deep in the money. The second transaction is purchasing in the money calls at a strike price that is higher than the one established for the calls you have already executed.

You need to write calls that are as far out of the money as possible for the 3rd transaction. The 4th transaction is purchasing out of the money calls with a strike price lower than the previous out of the money calls you have already written.

Each set of transactions involving the sale and purchase of calls must contain the same number of options contracts. They should be based on the same underlying asset expiring on the same date.

As with the short butterfly spread, the only decision you are left with is to decide the strike price. The strike price determines your profitability. The greater the difference between the strike prices and the existing market value of an underlying asset, the higher the residual profitability.

If the range of the strike prices is placed close together, it is known as an albatross spread.

Reverse Iron Butterfly Spread

While using this strategy, there are four simultaneous transactions you need to execute. You need to write and purchase calls and put options.

The first transaction is to write out of the money call options. The second transaction has to purchase and add the money call options. While you do this, you need to purchase and add the money put options.

The final transaction is to write out of the money put options. All the number of options contracts in each set of calls and puts executed is the same; they are all based on the same underlying security and share the same date of expiration.

Reverse Iron Condor Spread

The Reverse Iron Condor spread includes simultaneous transactions designed to improve your profitability during volatile market conditions. The first set of transactions involve purchasing out of the money put options.

The second set of transactions require you to sell out of the money put options at a strike price lower than the one you have already established while purchasing the options in the previous step.

The 3rd set of transactions involve the purchase of out of the money call options. While you do this, you need to sell out of the money call options at a higher strike price than the ones you have set for out of the money call options already purchased. Once again, the total number of contracts executed for each set of purchase and sale must be the same.

They are based on the same underlying asset and expire on the same date.

Now that you are aware of various trading strategies available, regardless of the market conditions, all that is left for you to do is improve your understanding.

Practice is the only way to test your knowledge and understanding. Don't worry; you don't have to start trading with your hard-earned money. Most option trading platforms these days have a demo account. Don't forget to check this feature and practice.

Chapter 11: Selecting Options to Trade

Now that you are aware of all the different trading strategies that can be used while trading options based on your outlook, let's move on to the next aspect of trading: learning to select the right options. Since there are different types of options and several underlying financial assets, making the right choice can become a little tricky.

From dealing with stocks of specific companies to commodities, currencies, and other financial instruments, the choice is overwhelming. Each of these financial assets has varying expiry dates and strike prices, and a calculated choice is necessary if you want to make the right decision.

In this chapter, you will get a few simple suggestions that can be implemented while selecting options to trade.

Investment Goals

Before you start trading, take some time and consider your investment objectives or goals. Ask yourself what you want to attain from trading. What are you looking for? What is the result you desire? Why do you want to trade in options?

Do you want to invest in options to diversify your portfolio? Or are you interested in learning how options trading works? Do you want to invest in options because you want to speculate the movement of the value of underlying assets? Do you want to trade in various commodities?

Whatever your reason is, you need to know it and underline it. This reason needs to be good enough and meaningful. Unless these conditions are fulfilled, your ability to make good decisions reduces.

These conditions also act as guidelines for every trade you make. So, be aware of your investment objectives first. Once you know what you desire from trading, selecting the right option becomes easy.

Risk Tolerance

The simplest way to understand your risk tolerance is by checking the reward and risk ratio. To determine your risk tolerance, ask yourself what the maximum loss you can sustain is. The answer to this question will determine your risk ratio.

For instance, a conservative investor wouldn't have a high-risk tolerance. An aggressive investor might be quite comfortable speculating in volatile market conditions, while a conservative one would stay away from situations like these.

It's not just your outlook towards the market that matters; your usual philosophy towards risk tolerance is equally important.

Implied Volatility

You cannot ignore the significant role played by implied volatility in the options market. Before you start investing, spend some time doing the groundwork.

Compare the levels of implied volatility teams for different options based on the historical volatility of underlying assets. Implied volatility gives you better insight into the general attitude of traders towards a specific option in the market under the existing circumstances.

If the implied volatility is high, the premium associated with such options will automatically be higher, making it an attractive investment. If the implied volatility is low, the premium will be low too. If you are interested in purchasing options, a low premium is something to look for.

On the other hand, if you are a seller, look for higher premiums. Your decision-making ability becomes better when you pay attention to the volatility of the options and the market in general.

Different Events

Stop paying attention to stock-specific and general market events when selecting the right option. All these events essentially affect the value of different financial instruments in the market at any given point in time. Any event that affects the entire market is known as a market-wide event. Whether it's the publication of a company's financial data or the changes in interest rates, these events affect how the entire market functions. Similarly, certain events are quite specific and affect only certain underlying assets.

For instance, the earnings report of a company or information associated with a specific commodity will affect the value of the options. These events can affect the implied volatility of the options traded in the market. It also influences the attitude of traders towards the market and the options. You must consider all these factors because they influence the options price.

Create a Strategy

If you have followed all the different suggestions mentioned until now, you have an elaborate analysis of the market in front of you. Now you are aware of your investment goals, risk and reward levels, implied volatility, and key events that affect different underlying assets in the market.

Selecting a specific option strategy becomes easier when you are aware of all these things. For instance, a conservative investor with a significant stock portfolio wouldn't mind writing covered calls on all the stocks in his portfolio to increase profitability.

On the other hand, an aggressive investor with a significant level of risk tolerance wouldn't mind buying puts on major stock indices.

By following the steps discussed in this chapter, it will become easier to find suitable options for your portfolio. A common denominator in all the suggestions is the need for planning. Without any planning and preparation, don't jump into options trading.

Chapter 12: How to Select a Broker

You might be quite excited to start implementing everything you have learned so far. But, before you start trading in the market, you need a broker. A broker is your only access to the market.

When it comes to selecting one, you need to be careful because they will be your solid investment partner. A quick Google search will lead to hundreds of results. How do you choose, and how do you know you have made the right choice?

These are the two questions beginners are usually scared of before trading options. However, you can put these fears to rest because here are five simple tips you can use to select an ideal broker.

Learning Opportunities

When it comes to selecting the right broker, you need to find one who offers free educational resources and tools. Learning is an important part of becoming an options trader. Regardless of whether you are just getting started or have been in the market for a while, learning will do you no harm.

The more information and knowledge you have, the higher the chance you will make better decisions. Always look for a broker who offers resources designed for educating their customers. Free education could be in any form. Whether it's a recorded webinar, face-to-face meetings, or personal guidance over the phone, look for education and guidance options.

An additional feature of a good brokerage is when they offer a demo account or online simulations for users to test their knowledge.

Now, you might wonder what the point of learning all this is if the broker will place the trades for you? Well, it is your hard-earned money at stake. It is advisable to use the broker's guidance and suggestions to make trades. That said, you should also be aware of exactly where your money is going and whether the trades are profitable or not.

Customer Service

An important aspect of selecting the right broker is the customer service they offer. This is important for all traders. You need to be high on their list of priorities, or it doesn't make any sense to pay that brokerage. Regardless of whether you are trying to learn more about a specific trade or want to make a trade, customer service matters. Consider the type of communication you prefer.

Do you want to communicate with your broker through online chat, email, phone calls, or any other means of communication? Do they have a trading desk whenever you need it? Does the brokerage offer 24/7 customer support and Technical Support? What are their operating hours and when can you call the broker? Who will answer your questions?

Before you select a broker, ask them all these questions. You can also check their Google reviews before making a decision. A little background check goes a long way if you want to become a successful trader.

Tools and Resources

To become a successful options trader, be prepared to do plenty of research and groundwork. Data will become your lifeline. While selecting a broker, there are certain basics you need to look out for, such as the charting services they offer, which lets you select entry and exit points for trades.

Make sure they have a court feed for different options which is frequently updated, tools to help you when analyzing potential risks and trades, and screening tools. Depending on the strategies you use, you need different types of tools, including analytical ones like customizable screeners.

You also need to create common tests and track the different strategies to ensure you have the right ones in place. Trading in real-time is quite different from learning and reading about it. Look for a brokerage platform that offers virtual or simulated training.

Before registering with a specific broker, ensure they offer all the services you are looking for. While doing this, make sure the different tools have common resources and whether the data they are offering is free or chargeable. You need to consider all the costs and charges involved before selecting a brokerage or broker.

Trading Platform

A quick Google search will list all the different types of trading platforms available. With the ever-increasing popularity of options trading and the advent of the Internet, online trading has become a breeze. The growing demand means the availability of online platforms has also increased.

So, it's important to find the right trading platform. Some can be accessed only on desktops, while others are compatible with mobile devices. Some offer software-based trading, while others are web-based trading. Some can also be a combination of everything.

While selecting a broker, carefully go through their business website and check the trading platforms they offer and their features. While doing this, check the tools and resources associated with each platform. If they offer any simulated trading, go through it and spend some time exploring all the features.

Apart from this, don't forget to read through testimonials and check any tutorial videos they have on the platform. When it comes to selecting the light-

trading platform, here are some factors you should consider.

- How easy is it to use the trading platform?

- Is the platform user-friendly?

- Does the platform have all the different features you are looking for? For instance, you might want a platform that lets you fill out a trading ticket that can be submitted later.

- Does the trading platform offer mobile access to its full site, or do you have to access it through your desktop?

- What is the reliability of the website, and how quickly do they execute the orders?

- Does the broker charge a specific fee? Is the fee monthly or annually?

Apart from all these different factors, another important consideration you cannot overlook is the balance maintained in the brokerage account. Do they have a minimum account balance, or does the brokerage account come with a specific limit of transactions that need to be conducted within a given period?

Being prudent and doing the required research will save you a lot of trouble in the future. What is the point of spending your money and hiring a broker who doesn't meet any of your training requirements? So, be a prudent trader and investor.

Commission Payable

Perhaps one factor that everyone looks at while selecting a broker is the commission payable. When it comes to selecting a broker, finding someone reliable is better than someone who doesn't charge commission.

There is no sense in investing in a broker if you cannot profit from them. At times, the costs are combined, and the trading commission also includes a per-contract fee, which is essentially a single fee payable per transaction. The per-contract fee and the base rate are two components required to calculate book commission payable. The base rate is the same as the trading commission and is payable by the investor whenever they trade any instrument in the market.

The contract fees usually charged by brokers can range from anywhere less than a dollar to hundreds or more. So, read through the commission payable carefully.

Certain brokerage accounts also require you to maintain a minimum balance with them. At times, other accounts require you to perform a specific number of trades within a given time period, according to which the commission is charged. If you are just getting started with options trading, it's always better to find a broker who charges a single flat fee for trade.

If you definitely follow all the different considerations and suggestions in this chapter, you will find the right broker in no time!

Chapter 13: Before Entering a Trade

Before you start executing any trade, you need to be aware of a few things. In this chapter, you will learn about all the different conditions and considerations to keep in mind before you make a trade.

By doing this, you are essentially filtering out all poor trade decisions, so you will be left with only the good ones.

Start With a Balanced Portfolio

The importance of having a well-balanced portfolio has been repeatedly mentioned in this book. Before you decide to add a specific instrument or investment to your portfolio, ask yourself why you want to add it?

Do you need it, or are you mimicking other traders? If your portfolio were primarily bullish, it would be better to not limit yourself. By doing this, you are essentially mitigating your risks.

If the market takes on bearish tendencies, all your bullish strategies will amount to nothing. The idea is to try and limit your risk in all situations. By balancing your trades, you can have better control over your portfolio's risk exposure. Bearish traders can add a few bullish strategies to offset the loss and mitigate risks and vice versa.

Liquidity

One of the most important qualities of a good option is its liquidity. Regardless of how attractive and lucrative an option looks, it doesn't matter if it is illiquid. This is one of the reasons why you must be prudent when selecting options.

For instance, if the underlying stocks are trading more than 100,000 shares daily in the market, it is a liquid option. If the numbers are too low, the trade isn't liquid and not worth your time and effort.

As a beginner, learning to pay attention to the liquidity of options and their underlying securities is a good habit to learn. Without liquidity, the contract doesn't amount to much.

Implied Volatility

Check the implied volatility of the options you want to trade. If it is relatively high, its premiums will automatically increase too. On the other hand, if the implied volatility is relatively low, the premium reduces.

Selling at a higher premium and buying at a lower premium is usually a profitable strategy. Similarly, at times, implied volatility can be used to predict how a specific option might do in the market in the future.

If you believe the implied volatility of an instrument will increase in the future, the trading strategies employed will be different from the ones used if the price reduces.

Select a Strategy

When it comes to trading options, selecting a good strategy is important. Picking a strategy is so much more than eliminating the one you don't want to use.

It's more about eliminating a bunch of strategies once you are aware of how the stock or the underlying asset works in the marketplace, its implied volatility, and the liquidity.

By considering all the different aspects of options pricing, picking the right strategy based on the market outlook and conditions becomes easy. Remember, there is no rule that says you should just pick one strategy.

If you want, diversify your portfolio and invest based on varying strategies to reduce your risk exposure.

Personal Trading Style

As with their usual outlook in the market, paying attention to your trading style is also important. It essentially determines the trades you decide to make in the market.

Some are risk-averse, while others don't mind taking on bigger risks. Any strategy you select must be one you are OK with in regards to the risk you are exposed to. The risk should not be more than what you can stand to lose.

Let's assume that you are selling credit spreads in the market. While doing this, you have the option to sell them at a strike price which gives you a 90% success rate or a 65% success rate. Now, the one with 90% success rate does not offer rewards as high as those offered by the 65%.

In this case, it is entirely up to you to decide which level of success and risk you are comfortable with. It must always fit your trading style and financial goals. Another thing you must do is give yourself sufficient time to make a good trade.

Of course, this does not mean waiting too long and missing opportunities, but really study the trade and everything about it just to make sure you're ok with whatever risk is involved.

Position Size

Position sizing is extremely important. Even veteran traders often overlook it. It's crucial to understand this aspect because it can make all the difference between a good and bad trade. Before you make a trade, assess opposition size. Trading bigger positions increases the risk you are exposed to, and you cannot overlook this.

If your position size is rather big and the trade doesn't go your way, the loss you incur also increases significantly. As a beginner, it is always better to start with small positions before moving on to bigger ones. Don't assume a big position in the market unless you are extremely comfortable with it and confident about how the trade plays out.

The Future

Trading options, regardless of whether it's a short or long-term option, involves future predictions. You cannot trade options without thinking about the future. Have you ever seen a test match between grandmasters?

It's believed grandmasters are capable of predicting up to 20 moves their opponent might make. This is their secret to success. Now, it is not possible to predict exactly how the future will unfold, but you can create different plans to reduce your risk exposure and mitigate potential losses.

Always have a plan in case your first one doesn't work out. Shielding yourself from potential losses is important to preserving your capital without hurting your earnings.

At times, regardless of how hard you try, it is not possible to always make good trades. That's just how the market works. Some trades might go wrong regardless of how good your strategy is.

However, continue learning from all these trades, reduce the scope of making mistakes, and make adjustments or formulate new plans to keep going.

Chapter 14: Mistakes to Avoid

The best way to learn and grow in life is through experience. Unless you try, you will never know. To improve your chances at success, learning to reduce the scope of mistakes is important.

At times, you can learn a lot from the mistakes others have made. Even though experience is the best teacher, learning from others' experiences is an equally good idea. In this chapter, you'll be introduced to the common mistakes beginners make when entering options trading.

Acquiring Out of the Money Calls

Purchasing out of the money call options is a part of several trading strategies, but if all you do is keep purchasing them, trading becomes slightly difficult. This is especially true for new investors.

Trading and out of the money calls are considered the trickiest means of investment, especially in the options market. They might be appealing because they are offered at low premiums, and you might also believe it's a good idea to try and select the profitable out of the money call options.

If you have ever traded equities, trading and calls will seem like an appealing option because the traits made are quite similar in both situations. Equity traders are used to purchasing low and selling high, and this is the same strategy one might use while purchasing out of the money call options. The significant disadvantage of this trading strategy is it exposes you to significant losses, and it reduces portfolio diversification.

A simple way to offset the risk exposure is by selling out of the money call options on stock you already possess. This is also known as a covered call. You were introduced to different types of covered calls in the previous chapter.

A wonderful thing about using this strategy is it reduces the risk of selling and the money call option because both positions you hold in the market are covered.

Whenever you are increasing your risk exposure by using a specific strategy, don't forget to offset this by using another strategy.

For instance, if you are using primarily bullish strategies, adding a few bearish ones to the mix will lower the risk. It's always important to diversify your portfolio when looking to mitigate risks, increase profitability, and reduce the scope of losses.

Always Have an Exit Plan

Most traders often consider creating elaborate strategies while entering and trading in the options market. However, it's not just important to know when to enter a market or how to make a trade;

understanding how to exit is equally important. If you don't have an exit strategy in mind, it simply increases the risk of losses you incur.

However, planning an exit strategy does not mean you are cutting your losses. If things don't work out according to your plan, if the market is unfavorable, or if there is no way to earn a profit, having an exit strategy in place will help.

Regardless of how brilliant a trade is, you need to have an upper and lower limit for closing. At times, the trade might seem to be going well, and you might be encouraged to double down and hold your position for longer. You should not only have specific values but a timeframe within which you need to enter and exit the market too.

When it comes to trading options, the market is subject to time decay, and unless you consider it, your trades will not be profitable.

For instance, let's assume the limits for exit markets are a loss of $20 and a profit of $40. Whenever a transaction hits either of these limits, you must automatically exit. This ensures your emotions are regulated, and they are not guiding your decisions.

Remember, planning or having an exit strategy on hand doesn't mean you are cutting your losses. If you want to be profitable and successful, you cannot ignore the importance of an exit strategy. Apart from the entry and exit points, you must also have a specific time frame in mind. This dictates when you should exit the market and not just enter.

Options are subject to time decay, and the value reduces as the expiry date approaches. If you hold onto a long call or put option believing the market will improve, but it doesn't, it's better to cut your losses than wait and incur greater losses later.

Liquidity

Whenever you receive any quote for the options you wish to trade, you will realize there is a stark difference between the asking and bid prices.

The bid price is the value someone else is willing to pay for a specific option and refers to the value of the buyer who doesn't mind spending to acquire a specific option.

On the other hand, the asking price is the value quoted by the seller to sell an option. The real value of the option is never represented by the bid price and usually lies somewhere between the bid and ask prices. The differentiation and value between them are determined by the liquidity of the option you want to trade.

Liquidity means sufficient active buyers and sellers are interested in trading in a specific instrument, and there is fierce competition in the market. This activity increases the bid and ask price of the options. When compared to stock markets, options markets are not as liquid. This is because stock traders usually trade using one stock while those in options trade are based on several different underlying assets with different expiry dates and strike prices.

Liquidity in the stock market is certainly higher than options. If the underlying security is inactive, the options contracts based on it will become inactive too.

This increase is the difference between the bid and the ask prices. Let's assume the bid and ask price for a specific option are $3 and $3.25, respectively. The difference of 0.25 might not seem much, but if you look at it again, you will realize the differences are rather massive (almost 10% of the underlying asset's actual value).

If a specific stock is traded or trades at least 100,000 shares on any given day, it is liquid. If an option contract is based on these stocks, it will be a liquid contract.

While trading in options, ensure the options you are looking for have at least an open interest of 50 times higher than the contracts you desire to trade. For instance, if you are trading 10 contracts, the open rate of interest considered acceptable or reasonable is 500 contracts.

Don't Double Down

In the stock market, doubling up is a strategy that might work, but in the options market, it does not.

Options are derivatives, and their value depends on the price of an underlying asset or stock they represent.

Properties of the options contracts are seldom the same as one of the underlying stocks they are based on. By compounding your total risk, you can reduce the contract cost for any position in the market. If the trade becomes unfavorable, don't double down on your position.

Ask yourself whether this is the same trade you would make if you were not holding on to the existing position or place in the market. If you believe this is not be the trade you would make, do not execute the additional option.

Close the trade altogether and look for another opportunity since this is always a better idea than trying to pump more money into an existing situation, believing you can improve it.

Multiple Trades

Now that you are aware of all the different advanced strategies applicable in varying markets and conditions, you realize they have a common point. Most advanced strategies are based on multiple trades made in the options market.

In a trade like this, multiple transactions must be executed simultaneously to attain a specific position in the market. The upfront costs people cover if you execute individual transactions will be higher than executing multiple ones. If the value of an underlying asset runs out before establishing your position, you are simply increasing your portfolio's exposure to risks.

Executing multiple trades is important to understand all the different positions you will be simultaneously opening and closing. Unless you get the hang of wanting to enter and exit the market and the trade you are making, you cannot get ahead.

Misunderstanding Leverage

A common factor most beginners fail to consider is the leverage options offered. If you are not aware of the leverage they offer or misunderstand it, your risk levels increase.

It is one of the most common strategies used by the big boys to purchase short-term calls. If that's the case, it's important to understand whether it's a speculator or conservative strategy.

The simplest way to determine whether you have chosen the right strategy or are trading with the right options is to start small. Start by trading 100 shares, and stick to one option.

If you want, you can also trade 300 share lots or three contracts. This is a good number to start with. If it does not pan out with one or three options contracts, it's highly unlikely that a bigger position on these trades is viable.

Not Trying New Strategies

Learning something new is seldom easy. It can also be quite intimidating, especially when your finances are involved. That said, unless you try, you will never know. This is where most beginners make mistakes.

If you find a strategy that works for you, it can be quite tempting to stick with it to turn out to be even bigger returns. Unfortunately, you cannot become a successful trader with just one strategy.

You need to learn how to apply different strategies as well, and the best way to do this is by implementing them. Lack of experimentation when it comes to trying new strategies can reduce your overall profitability.

Waiting Too Long

Waiting too long to buy back short options is a big trading mistake. You should always try to buy back short options as soon as you possibly can, in order to become successful.

Beginners usually make the mistake of waiting too long to buy back the options they have sold. There can be different reasons to do so. Maybe you believe the contract will be worthless upon expiration, or you want to earn more profits from that specific trade, or you are not interested in paying the commission. Whatever the reason is, it's simply delaying the buyback of the shares you have short sold.

As a rule of thumb, if you cannot retain 80% or more of the initial profit from the sale of an option, buy it back. If you don't, it means you have waited too long. Therefore, the risk increases.

Not Considering Upcoming Events

Several events in life are unpredictable, especially external factors. However, whenever you are trading options, there are two factors you should always pay attention to: dividend dates with the underline stock and the earnings from the underlying stock.

For instance, if you sell call options and the dividend date is approaching, chances are you will probably be assigned to the option early if it is in the money. This might happen if the dividend expected is rather large.

Option owners have no rights towards the dividend payable on an underlying stock. As the holder of an option, if you want to collect the dividend, you need to exercise your option and purchase the underlying shares. So, you need to ensure you are aware of all the upcoming events in the market.

Chapter 15: Managing Emotions

If you want to become a successful trader, it's important to learn to control your emotions. This is one aspect of trading most traders commonly overlook.

Emotional control is important in all aspects of your life, and especially more so when investing. Regardless of the investment or instrument you are trading in, managing your emotions can make all the difference between profit and loss.

How you interpret the prevailing conditions in the market, along with your perspective towards new opportunities, will be regulated by your emotional state.

For instance, if you are having a bad day at work, are frustrated about a specific unresolved issue, or anything else along these lines, these emotions will cloud your perspective. In turn, chances are that you will not be making good decisions. If you are not careful, you might end up wiping out your entire balance.

That being said, controlling your emotions is and cannot be stressed on enough. In the chapter, we offer different suggestions that you can use to do this and make smart decisions while trading.

Fear of Missing Out

We all have a fear of missing out. If you let this regulate your investment decisions, you are in for a lot of trouble. Learning to overcome this fear is an important skill.

There will be times when you are frustrated or annoyed because you believe you could not leverage a specific opportunity to increase your profitability while others seem to be doing well. This will happen at one point or another. In fact, it is better you prepare yourself for it.

Resisting the temptation to act on your impulses and learning to control these is important. Every decision you make about a trade needs to be a business decision. You can be passionate about trading, but don't let this cloud rational thinking and solid decisions. Wait for the right time to enter and exit the market.

There will be times when it feels like the market is steadily growing, and it's okay to hold out on opposition for a while longer.

However, if all the evidence points otherwise, go with it. Learning to cut your losses is as important as holding onto the opposition. If it feels like the trade you made is not going to improve, let it go.

Learn to Be Patient

Carefully consider all the different strategies we've discussed so far, as well as your general outlook towards the market, and understand your financial motives. Once you are aware of all these, select a trading strategy based on them.

And after selecting a strategy, don't be stubborn about it. Be flexible and patient while making your trades. If the market conditions are not favorable for the specific strategy you have in mind, change it.

Don't abandon your strategy because others seem to be doing something different than you. As long as you have spent the time required to weigh the pros and cons of a strategy, let it guide your decisions. Trading is about improving your financial health and not reducing your capital.

Be Willing to Learn

Do not let pride, ego, or any other narcissistic emotion prevent you from learning. It is okay to make mistakes. Similarly, it is okay to accept that you don't know everything about trading.

As long as you are willing to learn, you will grow as an investor. Try to spend around 15- 20 minutes a day learning more about the options market. The more you know, the better equipped you are to make profitable decisions.

Learn something new every day and do not only concentrate on a theoretical understanding of concepts. Apply what you've learned and practice.

There will be trades that are extremely profitable while others will not pan out. Regardless of the outcome, do not let these emotions get to your head. If you become overconfident about certain trades and refuse to change your strategy despite the market conditions, you will be digging your own grave.

Instead, consider all your trading decisions carefully and rationally. Strategic thinking and planning go a long way. And if you make a trading mistake, don't break down and think it's the end of the road. Mistakes give you opportunities to learn and, therefore, treat them as such.

Try to avoid the same mistakes in the future, maintain a positive mindset and keep learning!

A Sense of Direction

A common mistake most traders make is they don't have a proper sense of direction. Don't start trading just because you believe you need to. Don't rush into trading; instead, consider it to be another business decision. The only way to increase your profitability while mitigating unnecessary risks is to create a plan of action to achieve your financial goals.

Every trade is an important business decision that drains your resources. Unless you learn to make the most of these resources, you cannot get ahead as a trader. For instance, if you believe your trade is not going to be profitable, instead of doubling down on the position and hoping it will turn out better, let it go.

As mentioned, do not let your emotions guide your decisions. Let your business plan, coupled with the strategy chosen, guide you. Start thinking of all the trades you make as steps toward attaining your financial goals, and look at the bigger picture instead of the immediate results.

Don't Rush

Whenever you are executing a trade, don't be in a rush. You might be tempted to increase your profitability by holding on to the position when others are exiting the market.

If you believe your strategy will pay off, hold onto it for a while longer.

It takes conscious effort and practice to regulate your emotions. Learn to become aware of what you are feeling and be smart about how these emotions fit in the reality of the world around you.

Unless you do this, you will not be able to judge the market conditions properly.

In the previous chapter, you were introduced to different trading strategies based on the market outlook. Since your emotions regulate your outlook, it is important to regulate your emotions first. If you let your emotions govern your financial decisions or trading choices, you risk losing your hard-earned money.

Chapter 16: Risk Management

There is a certain degree of risk involved in every aspect of life, and trading is not any different. Even if there are different factors beyond your control, certain things can be regulated. You are free to determine the level of risk you are willing to take and your overall risk exposure.

Management of capital along with risk regulation is important when trading options. And when it comes to investing, regardless of the investment instrument, risk cannot be avoided. It's also said that greater risks result in better rewards.

However, exposing yourself to unnecessary risks is seldom desirable. Ensure you are trading with the capital that you can afford to lose. Stretching yourself thin financially for the sake of one trade is not recommended.

In this section, you will learn about the different tactics you can use for risk management in options trading.

A Trading Plan

The best way to manage risk exposure is by creating a trading plan. You need to have a plan and place for all the trades you want to make. This plan should be based on your financial goals, general outlook toward the market, and the strategies you want to use.

Failing to plan is planning to fail; always remember this mantra while trading. Your plan gives you the required guidelines and parameters while performing any trades in the market.

It needs to provide details about the capital you wish to use, the risk you are willing to assume, and your entry and exit positions. This ensures your funds are not misappropriated while your resources are optimally utilized.

Start with financial management to create your trading plan. The first step is to determine the laws or risk you are willing to expose yourself to by setting a 1 percent limit for all your trades.

It essentially means you should never place more than 1 percent of your total trading capital on any given trade. If you have $2000 in your trading account, you shouldn't trade more than $20 on any options contract. This ensures you are consciously investing within your means.

Different Orders

An effective and efficient means to regulate your risk exposure and options trading is by utilizing different orders. When it comes to options trading, you can buy puts, sell puts, sell calls, and buy calls.

You can use the same strategy not just for the contracts you execute but also for your opening and closing positions in the market. Risk management becomes easier when you start doing this. Clearly, all the different types of strategies you need in order to execute different orders were discussed in the previous chapters. You simply need to go through them and practice, and eventually, you will get the hang of it.

Any usual market order is fulfilled at a price that is best available at the time of its execution. There is a great way to buy or sell options in the market.

If the market is volatile, your order might be fulfilled at a price that is either higher or lower than the price you expected. By limiting your orders, you can establish maximum and minimum prices at which orders must be fulfilled. It also ensures you're not buying or selling options at unfavorable prices.

Diversify the Portfolio

A simple yet brilliant way to limit risk is by diversifying the portfolio. This essentially means investing in different types of instruments to offset losses from one with another. Basically, don't put all your eggs in one basket.

Regardless of the investments, you are trading, after all, and diversification is always recommended. If the investments you make are associated with multiple industries, sectors, companies and include diversified financial and management sectors, the risk involved decreases.

For instance, instead of investing all your capital in the stocks of a single company, invest in different companies. Also, be sure the companies belong to different sectors. Even if one sector crashes, your investment is protected while your losses are limited to single investments. Similarly, use different strategies while trading and don't stick to just one.

Automate Orders

Automate your option order so that you exit a specific position during certain market conditions. Before you start investing and trading, be sure to have an exit plan.

At times, it's better to cut your losses and exit instead of waiting for things to change for the better. You can do it manually, but automating helps save time and effort. It also reduces the risk of lapse and conscious decisions. Set a specific profit limit you want to earn or a loss you can sustain in any situation. After this, create an exit limit.

It essentially means you will exit the market as soon as a profit or loss limit has been attained. This is why automating orders is a good idea. For instance, if you believe the maximum gain sustainable on any trade is $5000, the exit point for you is $5000. If the investment hasn't reached this level or the market is unfavorable, your position will automatically be terminated.

It's not only important to know when to enter the market. Having an exit plan in place is equally important, and holding on to a position for too long, especially while trading options, can prove counterintuitive.

If you are not careful, even a good options contract can expire worthless because you forgot to exercise your right. Similarly, having an exit plan ensures you aren't incurring excess losses or holding a position for longer than desirable.

This helps avoid situations where you have missed out on an opportunity because you didn't react immediately. Option orders are the best way to limit your risk exposure while increasing profitability.

Your ability to regulate the risk depends on how well you are managing the funds available. These two concepts cannot be overlooked if you want to be a profitable and successful options trader.

Making the most of limited resources available, especially when there are multiple choices out there, is crucial. Ensure you stay levelheaded, favor rational thinking, and are prudent while utilizing the funds at your disposal to avoid unnecessary losses or high-risk exposure.

To increase your profitability, financial management is needed. Before you invest, have a specific capital budget for every trader to use. Even if one trade seems lucrative, but it is beyond your means, avoid it for now. While using a broker, short the orders you have created to prevent him from investing more than you want to invest in a specific trade. You can create an order where the broker cannot invest more than that specific sum in certain prevailing market conditions.

Conclusion

All the information you need to make better and smarter investing decisions while trading options are laid out in detail in this book.

From learning about the history of options trading, the benefits they offer, to the risks involved in developing a strategic plan and different strategies available while trading, this book will be your guide every step of the way.

The suggestions, tips, and advice given in this book are ideal for beginners. Apart from this, as you start your journey towards becoming an options trader, ensure you don't make the common trading mistakes discussed in this book and learn to manage your emotions while concentrating on risk management.

Once you are aware of all this, the only thing left is to start practicing and implementing the information you learned.

Don't forget to be patient while trading. Tread carefully and take your time before making any decisions. Once you get the hang of it, you will realize options trading is incredibly profitable and interesting.

Learn the different strategies, and make sure you have understood every aspect before implementing them.

When you do all this, you can certainly maximize your profitability and reduce the risks involved.

References

5 Things you must know Before Entering Futures and Options Trading | Motilal Oswal. (n.d.). Www.motilaloswal.com. https://www.motilaloswal.com/blog-details/5-things-you-must-know-before-entering-futures-and-options-trading/19936

A Brief History of Options | The Options Oracle. (n.d.). Https://theoptionsoracle.com/a-brief-history-of-options/

Bearish Options Trading Strategies - Trading in a Bear Market. (n.d.). Www.optionstrading.org. http://www.optionstrading.org/strategies/bearish-market/

Building a Balanced Portfolio with Options - DayTrading.com. (n.d.). Www.daytrading.com. https://www.daytrading.com/balanced-portfolio-options

Bull Market Options Trading Strategies. (n.d.). Www.optionstrading.org. http://www.optionstrading.org/strategies/bullish-market/

Burns, S. (2020, April 10). Risk Management For Options Trading. New Trader U. https://www.newtraderu.com/2020/04/10/risk-management-for-options-trading/

Corley, M. (n.d.). The Layman's Guide to Natural Gas Options - Part IV. Www.mercatusenergy.com. https://www.mercatusenergy.com/blog/bid/36919/The-Layman-s-Guide-to-Natural-Gas-Options-Part-IV

Davis, C. (2021, May 1). How to Choose an Options Trading Broker. NerdWallet. https://www.nerdwallet.com/article/investing/choosing-the-best-options-broker

Fernando, J. (2020, October 28). Energy Derivatives Definition. Investopedia. https://www.investopedia.com/articles/optioninvestor/07/energy_market.asp

History of Options Trading - How Options Came About. (2017). Optionstrading.org. https://www.optionstrading.org/history/

How To Trade Options - An Options Trading Checklist. (n.d.). Www.tastytrade.com. https://www.tastytrade.com/definitions/order-entry-checklist

Konchar, P. (2018, July 30). Trading Psychology: How To Control Emotions While Trading. My Trading Skills. https://www.mytradingskills.com/trading-psychology

Kuepper, J. (2019, August 19). Risk management techniques for active traders. Investopedia. https://www.investopedia.com/articles/trading/09/risk-management.asp

Mintz, J. (2020, July 7). Options Trading Terminology. Cabot Wealth Network. https://cabotwealth.com/lessons/options-trading-terminology/

Natural Gas Options Explained | The Options & Futures Guide. (n.d.). Www.theoptionsguide.com. https://www.theoptionsguide.com/natural-gas-options.aspx

Neutral Options Trading Strategies - Trading a Neutral Market. (n.d.). Www.optionstrading.org. http://www.optionstrading.org/strategies/neutral-market/

Picardo, E. (2020, April 19). Pick the Right Options to Trade in Six Steps. Investopedia. https://www.investopedia.com/articles/active-trading/111214/pick-right-options-trade-six-steps.asp

Risk Management and Money Management in Options Trading. (n.d.). Www.optionstrading.org. http://www.optionstrading.org/getting-started/money-management/

Top 10 Option Trading Mistakes: Watch How to Trade Smarter Now. (2019, January 25). Do It Right. https://www.ally.com/do-it-right/investing/top-10-option-trading-mistakes/

TradingStrategyGuides. (2020, October 29). Swing Trading Options Strategy for Steady Profits. Trading Strategy Guides. https://tradingstrategyguides.com/swing-trading-options-strategy-for-steady-profits/

Types of Options - Information on Different Options Types. (n.d.). Www.optionstrading.org. https://www.optionstrading.org/basics/option-types

Volatile Trading Strategies for the Options Market. (n.d.). Www.optionstrading.org. http://www.optionstrading.org/strategies/volatile-market/

Why Trade Options? - Benefits & Advantages. (n.d.). Www.optionstrading.org. https://www.optionstrading.org/introduction/why-trade/

Yochim, D. (2016, November 16). Options Trading Terms and Definitions. NerdWallet. https://www.nerdwallet.com/blog/investing/options-trading-definitions/